W9-BJQ-920

MY LIFE
IN
ASTROLOGY

MY LIFE
IN
ASTROLOGY

by Sybil Leek

PRENTICE-HALL, INC.
Englewood Cliffs, New Jersey

MY LIFE IN ASTROLOGY by Sybil Leek
Copyright © 1972 by Sybil Leek

All rights reserved. No part of this book may be
reproduced in any form or by any means, except for
the inclusion of brief quotations in a review, without
permission in writing from the publisher.

Printed in the United States of America   3

Prentice-Hall International, Inc., London
Prentice-Hall of Australia, Pty. Ltd., North Sydney
Prentice-Hall of Canada, Ltd., Toronto
Prentice-Hall of India Private Ltd., New Delhi
Prentice Hall of Japan, Inc., Tokyo

Library of Congress Cataloging in Publication Data

Leek, Sybil.
My life in astrology.

1. Astrology.
BF1408.2.L44A3   133.5'0924   72-37290
ISBN 0-13-608521-0

Third Printing........October, 1972

DEDICATED TO

Grandmother Louisa and her daughter, my
mother—"the other Louisa"
With love and gratitude for their help, understanding, and tolerance all through my life.

CONTENTS

MY LIFE IN ASTROLOGY

CHAPTER 1

Astrology—Passport to Living

Astrology is my science, witchcraft is my religion, and writing is my profession. Like most people, I have gone through periods of my life when I have seen myself as a complex personality, but during the years that brought me to the brink of the Aquarian Age, all the complexities have become unraveled. These few simple words really sum up the woman called Sybil Leek.

Astrology—the influence of the planets on all living things —has intrigued me since I first became acquainted with it as an eight-year-old child. Forty years later, I am no less fascinated by it, and hopefully I have learned something from it that has affected the structure of my life. Most of all, astrology has taught me tolerance and how to live a very eccentric, individualistic life in a world that is intolerant of anyone who does not completely conform to herd instincts by having both a public mask and a private face. Astrology shows the causes behind certain effects, and when one knows why certain people behave the way they do, their lives become predictable, and it is much easier to deal with difficult situations that arise. The horoscope is a chart for living, a magical document that opens the door to opportunity and shows strain and stress periods so that pitfalls can be avoided.

Many people have called me an opportunist, and all too often they have meant it in a derogatory sense. Yes, I am an opportunist, because I know how to turn advantages into positive expressions of different facets of my life. However, I do not simply wait for something to turn up. I make myself cognizant of the future, for opportunism is being aware of the right season for things, people, and places—and then pressing on. Basically, astrology is concerned with timeliness—the knowledge that there is a season to do all things. There is a greater ration of success when we acknowledge these seasons. Better not to go on a picnic if the weather forecast (an acceptable form of prediction today) indicates rain. If you must go on a picnic, at least make plans to carry a raincoat, wear the right clothing, and perhaps have an emergency refuge to go to when the prediction of rain fulfills itself.

More than ever before, I am aware of the need to time everything properly, and despite my success in many ventures and adventures of living, I have evolved through periods of trial and error. There is nothing wrong with making mistakes, if one does not continue to make the same mistakes over and over again. I am not really sure what *success* means, but I suppose it is the favorable termination or result of any affair. Many forms of success, but not all, are a measure of one's happiness as a human being. Certainly success has a price, and astrology has taught me how to analyze whether the price is likely to be worth the intangible costs. My chief success is being able to know myself for what I am. Millions of words have been written about me as a celebrity, an eccentric, a writer, a follower of witchcraft, an astrologer, and sometimes, though too rarely, as a human being seeking to the best of her ability to attain an harmonious existence in a world full of imbalances. The search for a balanced life has been my ambition: to know my virtues and vices, to try to balance them, and finally, through attaining this balance, to recognize my place in the universe as just one segment of a greater whole.

Self-analysis can play a great role in life, but it is not the total answer; neither is analysis done by a psychiatrist or psychologist, for we all cheat a little. Basically, we want to be "nice" people in order to be accepted in society; our morals and general behavior usually serve the same purpose. We may appear as a different type of person than we really are in order to conform to a code in business or to win the love of another person. But what really makes us tick can best be ascertained by astrology, because this science (as all sciences must be) is based on truth, the most elusive quality in any person's life. We cannot cheat in astrology if we set up a chart based on the day, month, place, and time of birth, because astrology is a series of mathematical progressions in which planetary patterns are considered in relation to each other. From the aspects of the angles made by the planetary patterns we can see how a personality should develop, how it will have the potential toward expressing itself, and, most of all, how the conscious and the subconscious merge to create the living human mechanism.

Sometimes we place too much credence on our mind, our body, or our emotions. Astrology teaches us that all these aspects make up the complete person. A man who is all mind is just as imbalanced as an overly emotional person, or one who places too much store on his tangible body. I am always amused at people who set so much store by the Sun sign. As an astrologer, I know that an assessment of anyone's life based entirely on the Sun sign is just so much moonshine. It's like giving a detailed analysis of the fingers of one hand and forgetting that the rest of the body matters, too.

The outer cover of the human body does not tell the whole story when viewed from outside. The body is simply a vehicle for the intangible qualities of the mind, spirit, and emotions. When we discover the intangible qualities of a person's life, we find out what he is really like. The need to produce an image that conforms with someone else's standards of expected behavior can make liars of us all. We seem to be living in a world that forces many of us to lose our identity. The world is changing, however, and we are witnessing a resurgence of man's primeval desire to know himself, his place in the world, and ultimately, the identity of his neighbors.

I see astrology as the most vital help in this process of identification, but it is a tool, not a religion or a panacea. It certainly should not be a crutch whereby the subject of a horoscope can blame the stars for his "bad luck." Astrology can only point out that there is really no such thing as "bad luck" meted out as punishment for our time on this earth. No evil fairy yearns to get even with us mere mortals, nor do the stars glare down balefully, or benevolently, on us. Life is a mixture of good times and times that are not so good, and more often than not, we can help ourselves by seeing obstacles not as problems, but as challenges. How we overcome the obstacles is the real measure of how successful we are. By indicating the best timing for events in our lives, astrology can help to eliminate the idea that bad luck is reserved for some people while others seem to have it easy. If you come to a puddle of water, you have the choice of going through it, jumping over it, or skirting around it. Your choice may be directed by your needs, wants, and desires. You may need to

keep clean because you are on the way to an interview for a
job or to meet someone you need to impress. You may want
to walk through it for the sheer sensation of walking through
water. You may desire to jump over it to prove you are
young and agile, or for any one of a number of reasons. The
point is, you have free will to do much more in life than you
may realize.

Free will matters, but we must never forget that its effi-
ciency and ability to work depends on the planetary patterns
at the time of birth, and then, as the life of the individual
goes on, by the transits made by the planets at specific times.
So many people are prone to excessive fear that they never
exercise their free will in anything. Others cannot exercise it
because they might hurt someone else. All too often, free will
is relegated into seeming nonexistence because of outside circumstances and pressures on our lives. It is sad to see so much
free will being used only to make mistakes. "My God, why
have ye forsaken me?" is not an uncommon sound to the ears
of an astrologer from a client bemoaning his "misfortune" to
all who will listen. As an astrologer with many years of experience, by now I am used to every attitude, from the dedicated
devotion of clients who have learned to take advantage of
their charts to those who want to hear only the good and
have no time or use for self-improvement. Astrology is more
than a mere fortune-telling device, however, because it aims
to help the subjects to know themselves better. This can be
done only by pointing out areas in which they may not be
fulfilling their potential because of neglect or an inability to
pursue a project to its end so that all its advantages can be
taken. Also, many people seem determined to become a
martyr to circumstances over which they have no control.

This penchant for martyrdom can lead to apathy, especially when the death of someone close to the person occurs.

One woman called me just after the death of her husband, and she was more distraught than anyone I had seen for a long time. I did not meet her at first, but I prepared her charts from details of the place, time, and date of her birth, which were given to me over the telephone. Despite frequent phone calls (which had more to do with her need to have a shoulder to cry on than anything else), she always spent a long time extolling the virtues of her past married life and trying to build up a picture of life as a constant bed of roses.

This was far-removed from anything I could see in the chart. She was born with the Sun in Libra, while the deceased husband was a Capricorn. She liked to spend money, but he had Saturn in Taurus, which always gave him anxiety about money. He had the capacity to earn through hard work, but with it came a fear of poverty, and consequently a desire to economize unjustly. His need to invest safely must have led to some friction, since it was in contrast to her profligate, typically Libran nature that loved to spend, and to her carelessness in all money matters, due to her own Neptune in Taurus. It was obvious that he could and would make money, and she could siphon it away as quickly as it was made.

He was coolly intellectual with his Moon and Mercury in Virgo, while she had her Moon in Scorpio and was very sexual and sensual. The combination of these qualities is no criterion for a truly happy relationship, much less an ideal married life.

It is not unusual for death to make a hero even out of a bad husband, especially to a romantic Libran wife left behind with not much more than a subdued guilt complex to sustain her. There were moments when I admired the lady for making the best of her marriage in retrospect, but I felt that she protested too much and might delude herself in the future. Suppose she carried on in idealizing the dead husband—what

chance had she of being able to recognize anyone else who
came along? We all know that comparisons can be odious.
Also, after many phone calls, I felt that she was enjoying the
martyrdom of widowhood.

Facing reality is generally distasteful, and this lady obviously had not faced it for many years; otherwise, she might
have seen that her attitude toward money perhaps had has-
tened her husband's death.

I discovered in her horoscope that she would marry again,
for she had Venus in Scorpio placed in a position where she
could hope to obtain financial success through married life.
When I told her this, to my surprise she screamed at me so
lustily that one would have thought I had suggested she
should go out and earn her living as a prostitute. Actually, I
think it was probably her reflex action against the idea of
marriage itself!

It is not unusual for me to find myself disliked for speaking the truth about what I find in various horoscopes, so she
was no exception. In between screams, I managed to tell her
that she would have the *opportunity* to marry again within
the next two years. Of course, she still had free will and could
turn down any proposal.

About eighteen months later, she arrived at my house in
Hollywood in a state of frenzied triumph to tell me that she
was still unmarried, and what did I think about that? Quite
gently I reminded her that there were still a few months to
go. I noticed that she was not quite so enthusiastic about the
virtues of her late husband, but was more inclined to moan
that she missed the status of being married, and she could not
understand why she had so little money. Also, she hated to
go out into any form of social life without an escort.

We arranged to have dinner together, but just as I was getting ready to keep the appointment, she called me to say she

felt ill, and it was canceled. About midnight, she called again, and she was obviously very agitated and sick. Being a stranger in Hollywood, she was afraid to call a doctor just by glancing through the yellow pages of the telephone directory. I recommended a man I had known for some time on a social basis; I had heard good reports about his ability. What started as a professional visit to a lady ill with food poisoning turned out to be a romance. I had forgotten that the doctor had lost his wife some six months earlier. Being of the Jewish faith, he preferred to wait to get married, and six months later I received an invitation to the wedding.

As I had already done the horoscope of the doctor and his previous wife, I could see from a comparison of the two horoscopes that they would be happy, and they are. Today we sometimes have lunch together, and we have quite a laugh about the grim period when the lady could not believe in her own destiny or her potential for achieving happiness. Fortunately, she now sees her previous marriage in a different light— less romantically, perhaps, yet aware that they had some good years together.

Years ago, when I was born, the stars hitched themselves to my wagon and helped speed me on my way, so that I touched the lives of hundreds of people and entered a wonderful world of magic moments and exciting adventures. Sometimes the stars alerted me to man's inhumanity to man, but they always made me aware that no human being is an island cut off from the source of life.

Yes, the planets were in pretty good aspect when I was born. As I move into old age, I feel that rare quality of being a totally free-spirited woman who was favored by the stars at her birth and was enabled to know that all human beings have magic in them. The secret is to know *how* to use this magic, and astrology is a vital tool for doing just that.

CHAPTER 2

Community Living—Family Style

No one could have had a happier childhood than I did, living in the midst of a family of unusual people who were lovable for their human qualities, and not simply because of the coincidence of birth that made us blood relations. Although I wrote extensively about my childhood in my autobiography, *Diary of a Witch*, I realize, when the veils of time lift from my memory, that I still have incidents left to tell. No matter where I am in the world, even when I am living an exciting life in a glamorous place, I realize that the people I knew in my childhood have had a lasting effect on me.

Our enormous household, with eighteen relations of varying ages, may sound like a nightmare to people today who live in small secluded units and sometimes seek to break all blood ties as soon as possible. It was communal living at its best. Everyone did whatever they had to do, but we always met for dinner in the evening. I suppose I was one of the most inquisitive children in the family; whatever was going on in the house, I wanted to know about it, and fortunately there was no segregation of children from adults. No one ever said, "Run away and play by yourself. I'm busy." My two pairs of great allies were my Irish grandmother and my father, and my mother and her sister, Celia. The allies in each pair of favorites were complete contrasts. My grandmother and father had spirited verbal sparring matches that should certainly not be construed as quarrels. My grandmother had a down-to-earth point of view about everything, while my father believed that an intellectual, academic form of reasoning was essential. She was the comely country-type witch, prepared for anything and able to give pronouncements of basic ancient wisdom. Only five feet tall, slim as a willow wand, she was also a fighting tigress in the way she approached religion, esoteric thinking, and metaphysics. She believed that attack was the best form of defense, and she would throw out statements with an attitude, "Now prove me wrong, if you can."

Few people could, but my father always felt that he had to try. He looked something like Don Quixote—very tall and very wiry. When he tangled with Grandmother, he knew he was tilting at a windmill. I think he also knew she was the greatest catalyst for his own mind, but in any case, they respected each other as worthy opponents. Their acceptance of reincarnation and their ability in astrology were cohesive forces that often united them as a stalwart bulkhead against the opinions of other people outside the family. Yet even in discussing these two areas, Grandmother maintained her down-to-earth attitude and Father remained the intellectual.

Grandmother never read a book on Hindu or Buddhist philosophy in her life, but my father could quote chapter and verse on anything. When Ralph de Tunstall Steele visited us, Grandmother was quite at home talking to him about his

Buddhist attitude. Ralph came from one of the oldest families in England, which traced its ancestry back to the Norman Conquest; his ancestors were present at the signing of the Magna Charta. Being southern Irish to the core, Grandmother preferred to forget these honorable antecedents and was much more certain that she and Ralph had been friends in a former life. Father understood all theories of "mind over matter," but he liked using experiments to prove that it worked. "Why go through all that paper work," Grandmother said, "when you can see mind-over-matter principles a work in everyday life?"

I had a springer spaniel called Roger. He was born when I was, and lived until we were both nineteen. Wherever I went, Roger followed, but occasionally he would go off on a foray of his own into the woods surrounding the house. He was trained to the gun because we had to rely a great deal on food brought in from the estate. (In English country houses, what the estate yields in game, fishing rights, vegetables, and fruits is vital to the upkeep of the household.) A careful retriever of game, Roger could carry an egg in his mouth, but I guess he liked to have a bit of private life, too. Whenever he wandered off about his own business, Grandmother liked to demonstrate that she could "call him home." She did not believe in going out into the woods after Roger, so she would quietly compose herself and literally *think* the dog home.

Although she would fight against it, Grandmother secretly enjoyed being asked to do experiments with my father. She had quite a few prima-donna instincts; she could always be persuaded to do anything she really wanted to do, but she would mutter loud enough for my father and his visitors to hear that "[she had] better things to do than to turn [herself] into a three-ring circus to entertain guests."

She certainly did have things to do and today I marvel

when anyone thinks that perpetual motion has not yet been established. Grandmother was a dynamo of energy until the day she died, at the age of ninety-eight. I see now how much time she devoted to me. No matter if she was supervising meals, delivering babies in her unofficial capacity as a mid-wife, making dresses, supervising the herb garden and vege-tables, or taking a long walk in the country—she always had time for me. She gave me my basic knowledge of astrology, with an emphasis on the personality traits and the psychology of people, while Father gave me the technical knowledge of how to set up a chart, taking meticulous care to be accurate in those basic calculations. Grandmother would draw the signs and symbols and the planetary aspects of the day on just about anything that was within reach, using a stick on the ground, a skewer on the pastry top of a pie, or a needle on a piece of embroidery. She would make a rough design and then wheedle my father into cutting out a template from which she could work.

She loved embroidery; consequently, I too became no mean hand with it. I still have massive pieces of embroidery that I did when I was a young girl. One of my most treasured ones is a huge bedspread. Grandmother sketched out dozens of herbs for this bedspread, and each herb was given to an aunt or a cousin to embroider. Each section was embroidered by a different woman in the family, with Grandmother's per-sonal work naturally dominating the centerpiece.

I was not only taught my basic astrology from symbols on pie crusts in the kitchen, but I also learned some basic herbal lore by watching my relatives engaged in the ladylike occu-pation of embroidery in the drawing room. Later in my life, my two sons found some of the old embroidery and also be-gan to make designs and templates, from which they created a small business called Leek's Magic Carpets. Many of their astrological rugs and carpets have appeared in art exhibitions and have been extensively photographed. Today, however, people seem to think it is a rare achievement for two boys to understand embroidery and rug-making. If Grandmother were around today, she would still see it as a very practical and necessary experience.

My mother was a contrast to her mother, and I watched her mix my grandmother's basic teachings with my father's intellectual quality. She still writes me the most exquisite letters in a handwriting that shows a beautifully balanced nature. An ardent theosophist, she has a special way of looking after children. I never met any child who could not get along with my mother, probably because they recognize the unusual maternal instinct in her. She seems to get right into the world of children, and now that I am older, I know the secret of this feat.of magic: she is a rare being who, despite her years, has maintained the remarkable quality that children lose too soon in life—a wide-eyed wonder. She is perhaps the only totally innocent person I ever met, who thinks no evil, and therefore knows no evil. People always ask me why I do not bring her to America, but I think it would be like transplanting a delicate, rare flower from a hothouse and expecting it to survive and grow in an alien wilderness. She leads what might be called a sheltered life, but this is the best life for her, one in which she can function in her special dedicated way. She always has children around her who learn to love her. Most of all, they trust her, just as I did when I was a child.

My grandmother danced through life, loving the limelight, and I lumber through my own life, accepting the limelight, too, but my mother does not need any boost to her ego. She knows how she must function, and she does her special best. Her mind is limitless in its appreciation of the wonders of nature, and next to nature, there are always children. Today she passes on more valuable knowledge to her little brood of grandchildren and their friends than any university professor is likely to do. If she is naïve about the brutality in the world today, it is because she has transcended the need to associate with violence and man's inhumanity to man. Her knowledge of astrology is limited, but she is rarely wrong in assessing personality traits by association with twelve signs. Her marriage to my father, a beautiful experience, seemed to fulfill the Platonic idea that a perfect marriage occurs when two ancient souls find each other and know themselves for what they are. She accepted my father's death with the true faith of a theosophist, knowing that the spirit within my father could not die and must always be entwined in her own life. Today she takes more interest in whatever I write about astrology, and she thoroughly approves of my growing interest in the written word as a vehicle to teach and help other people. She does not approve of what she calls "my racketing around America," but she accepts it as a part of my life.

Her influence on my two sons has been as great as the influence of my grandmother's on my life. When I came to the United States, I had no qualms at leaving them in my mother's capable hands. They both love and respect her; most of all, they have a healthy ability to tease her in a good-natured way, which she enjoys. They also know that she will do whatever she believes to be right and proper. Recently she surprised us all when she discovered that a chemical-warfare plant was operating very near Hampshire in England. She wrote to my eldest son to express her distaste, and she followed it up with a letter in which she said she was going to draw attention to this in no uncertain manner. Julian, with a dash of extrasensory perception, remarked that "Nana will be picketing the place in no time at all and trying to teach those scientists all about loving their neighbors." The next day we had a letter telling us that my sweet, innocent mother had quietly led a deputation of theosophists and Quakers to talk to the scientists.

Sometimes I think my family were the first to discover ecology, for we have always been so conscious that man must be part of his environment and must not despoil it. Any form of life survives only as long as it can successfully adapt itself to its environment. The environment is constantly changing in accord with the laws of the universe, but man has sought to override the principles of nature. An organism's failure to continuously adapt itself results in its dissolution. Similarly, the ability of a soul to adapt the organism it functions within depends upon the soul's powers of control. The more complete its control of its form—in part and as a whole—the more successful it will be in making the adaptations that are essential for physical survival.

The soul evolves progressively, step by step, as its experiences in controlling forms of limited functions gradually lead it to a state where it can control more complex forms. It finally incarnates in human form because it has won the power to control this most complex of all forms. Man's success in life depends solely on his ability to control the organism he occupies, and thereby adapt it to his needs. The vibratory rates in his astral form at birth indicate the natural power of control in different directions. If the Sun and Moon are strong and harmonious, it indicates his ability to attract many material advantages. Therefore, if he is born with a harmonious control, he can transmit and attract physical wealth as he chooses. He can exercise little control in those parts of his astral body that are weak and inharmonious unless he sets about systematically organizing other vibrations to nullify these weaknesses.

Astrological knowledge helps a person to systematically organize his vibrations properly. Health, for instance, results from harmonious vibrations that indicate a control of the motions of the astral form that attract health. Man has free will to debilitate both health and wealth. Modern man has befouled his environment so much that serious-minded people are wondering whether we can do anything to stop the decay in the world before it is too late. Man will stop the decay only when his spirit evolves at the same rate as his physical evolution. At some point, man lost touch with nature in his race to gain material possessions. A better knowledge and use of scientific astrology can help solve many of our ecological problems.

Survival, success, progress—all depend upon the ability of the soul to control the form it occupies and adapt it to its temporary needs for expression. It is in the loss of control of the spirit and the spiritual forces that we may well find the cause of man's inharmonious existence within the natural environment. The things we used to do years ago, such as husbandry of the land by the rotation of crops, became debilitated as we moved into the age of inorganic and chemical substitutes for food. Now we must adapt to a chemical way of life or find ways to combat it, if we are to survive.

My Aunt Celia is one of the best designers of ceramics I have ever known, and her love of nature comes out in all her work. While I can see my grandmother as an unusual human being, my mother as an archetype of innocence, I can only describe my aunt as "a good woman," who is more than kind to other humans. She ardently follows the ideals of my grandmother without getting too involved or bogged down in seriousness. Her main contribution to family life was her understanding of each individual, and she was very much a liaison among everyone in the family (not that anyone sulked or was indifferent to others). By reason of her age and wisdom, my aunt was a bridge between the young and old. She could always be relied upon, and not merely in emergencies, but for such things as seeing that the household pets were fed at the proper times. If we children were growing our own plants in our rooms, she was the one who took charge of their welfare in our absence.

The only thing she did not enjoy doing was looking after my frogs. I had a mania for collecting tadpoles from ponds, and I kept them until they grew up. Frogs produce their jelly-encased eggs (with little embryos that look like the symbol for Mars) in enormous quantities because, in their natural environment, frogs may have a high mortality rate because of all the creatures that prey upon them. But I could hatch and raise frogs with very little loss, defying all official statistics. (That Sun-in-Pisces aspect of my astrological makeup still makes me vastly interested in all forms of aquatic life.)

I had hundreds of frogs, and when they were big enough, I would take them back to the ponds around the house so they could go about their business of supplying next year's quota of jellied tadpoles. I would keep a few for personal pets, but in order to raise them efficiently, I had to use one of the bathrooms.

The idea of an English bedroom with its own bathroom was only a dream in my youth; I shared a bathroom with my aunt. The frogs, in turn, shared the bathroom with us. The bathtub was impressively enormous and had Doulton ceramic taps and a massive copper water heater that belched into life when a taper was applied to the gas jet. The bathtub was not really used as a breeding ground for the frogs, but the rest of the bathroom was. We had huge supplies of ewers and basins stored in the attic, and I would bring them down to serve as aquatic nurseries in the spring. Later on, when I ran an antique shop, these ewers and basins—many of them gorgeous examples of the potter's art—were sold to visiting Americans, who raved about them. I always wondered if they would have been surprised if they knew the quantity of small aquatic creatures their art treasures had once housed.

All the pet frogs were rehoused, ultimately, in a room we called our winter garden, which was a vast conservatory full of unusual plants. The room was heated by yards of hot-water pipes in the winter months to provide a lush, warm atmosphere for exotic house plants and a haven for those who wanted to enjoy them. Frogs—even if they do not always turn into handsome princes—are a valuable asset to a conservatory, since they keep down certain pests.

Aunt Celia dutifully learned to live with my frog farm, but when we had a new bathroom built in the house, she was the first to put in a plea for it. Two younger cousins moved in to share the old bathroom with me.

Celia, born with the Sun in Aquarius, was as interested in astrology then as she is today, but somehow we never seemed to have too many members of the family involved in the same pursuit at the same time. She was interested in numerology and phrenology, and she gave me my basic instruction in these two interesting subjects.

Personal instruction was always available right in my home, yet I never felt I was being specially instructed in anything, because studying was part of the way of life. No one sat down to listen to an adult lecture; rather, conversation moved from one subject to another, and the younger members of the family were encouraged to get involved. As I got older, I gradually decided for myself that astrology was for me, but I am glad I had some training in other areas. Everything integrates in the end, and there is really no division between any of the unusual subjects that were so much a part of my life as a

child. Astrology was, and is, my first love, but now I know
that there are links between astrology and numerology,
phrenology, palmistry, physiognomy, the laws of nature and
the universe, and ultimately the Old Religion, more commonly called witchcraft. This does not mean that all exponents of
the "-ologies" must find themselves involved in witchcraft. I
know many Presbyterian palmists, Methodist phrenologists,
and Roman Catholic numerologists, but the best ones have
a keen awareness of spiritual forces that is essential if a man
is to know himself and his relationship to the universe.

When I was eight years old, I already understood how to
set up an astrological chart, but it took many years for me to
understand all the permutations of a full and meaningful in-
terpretation. Hand in hand with learning how to set up a
chart went lessons in philosophy and psychology from my
father, and invaluable lessons from my grandmother about
health in relation to planetary patterns and influences. I still
think it is never too early or too late to learn about astrology.
The main requisite is a desire to understand the nature of
man and his place in the environment; for me, this desire
manifested itself early in life.

Of course, like most children, I loved to show off. Just as
some children today love to get up and recite a poem, so I
liked to make up a chart. In my three short years at school, I
had to learn to subdue this instinct, as I found I was dealing
with a subject that did not have the general appeal it has today. I would do my school friends' charts, but I was forbidden to try to give them any instruction, since the teachers in
the school, with the exception of the science mistress, felt it
might upset parents to think that their children were obtaining extracurricular knowledge in astrology. But children will
always do something that savors of being forbidden, and astrology was no exception. I would hold informal lessons, at

which about twenty children would congregate, in some quiet spot not on the regular patrol of the supervising teachers. Generally it was in one of the enormous bathrooms in the old country mansion that had been converted into our school. It's amazing how much basic astrology I taught, using the marble floor as a blackboard. All traces of our illicit lessons could quickly be erased by a frantic wielding of the towels and the huge natural sponges we used before the era of the decorative face cloth.

I always regret that we did not have astrology books in those days. So much could have been achieved by surreptitiously reading them under the bed covers in the dormitories. Many of us would have sacrificed the *Perils of Pauline* and *True Love* for a chance to read up on astrology.

The mayor of the local town had a daughter, Jean, who also attended the school as a day-scholar. She would have made a wonderful astrologer, but I doubt that she kept up with her studies once we parted company. We were united in a firm friendship because we were the only two redheads in the school, and together we weathered a storm of nicknames, such as "carrot top" and "freckles." We could always be identified when there was trouble at school. When we went for walks in the town, we tried to disguise our telltale red hair by sleeking it down with water or cold tea to make it look darker. (We only tried the cold tea once—it failed.)

We had the sort of freckles, too, that even the slight sunshine of an English summer caused to flare up into a cascade of unsightly brown blotches that no amount of cucumber salves could remove. Starting with lengthy, serious consultations about beauty, we finally became stalwart friends in other matters, including the study of astrology.

As the daughter of a local politican who had been on the town council and was now a distinguished city father, Jean

was naturally interested in civic affairs. Her father was also
the owner of the local paper for which I did some of my first
articles. I even got paid for them—the vast sum of three shil-
lings (half a dollar).

Our first big moment of fame as astrologers came when we
used astrology to work out the results of the local council
elections. Jean got the dates of birth, places, and times of
birth for all the candidates, and we wrote our own bulletin
some two hours before the official results were published.

Jean's father was set for victory with a nicely placed Sagittarius at his Midheaven, although the local opinion was that
he had his day and his opponent must surely win. Hope and
loyalty to the family were not enough for us, so we worked
hard on those charts—probably when we should have been
doing homework.

Our bulletin turned out to be right, and the headmistress
found out about it. She thought it savored more of black
magic than a mathematical progression of facts, and she had
no time to listen to our explanation that Sagittarius at the
Midheaven was just fine for winning elections that year.
After a feeble attempt to explain, we gave up and suffered
the inevitable "black mark" against our names. I think we
probably collected more black marks than anyone else. At
the end of the term, our school report showed how many
black marks we had, but not the reason why they were there.
I still think it was unjust to give black marks for being right
in astrology when someone else could get black marks for
much more heinous offenses, such as nearly blowing up the
science laboratory, which our good friend Katherine specialized in.

The practical aspect of punishment was more important to
us than the black mark. We had to do menial work in the
kitchen after everyone else had left the dining room. This cur-

tailed our walks on the grounds of the lovely old Elizabethan
house that was our school. Instead, we looked forward to a
week of gloomily scraping plates after the midday lunch and
being responsible for allowing only food scraps to get into
the large bins used for swill for the pigs kept on the school
farm.

From the first, I had no intention of doing this task, so we
devised a plan. I was always good at organization; indeed,
some of my present ability to be an opportunist stems from
my practice in school. We had so impressed our illicit astrology class with our Sagittarius-at-the-Midheaven prediction
that they became even more intrigued by the subject. The
time had come for me to cash in on our status and do my
first bit of trading. I managed to convince everyone that they
needed a *personal* horoscope, and in exchange for doing
everyone's personal horoscope, the class would take turns
scraping those dismal plates and seeing that the pigs were not
offended by anything passed on to them.

Two girls substituted for us after every meal. No two girls
had to do more than one meal, for there were enough astrology students to get through the entire week without repeti-
tive kitchen duties. Meanwhile, Jean and I worked quietly on
the horoscopes. They were crude, for we were not concerned
with projecting too much into the future; we merely concentrated on how each student would get through the next ex-
aminations. Everyone was very pleased. We felt we did a good
job, and most of all, we enjoyed being one up on our arch-
enemy, the headmistress. There were a few nervous moments
when girls not in the class discovered that we were getting
out of the kitchen chores. We could not bribe them to keep
quiet by offering to do their horoscopes because they were
not interested. The only alternative was to induce fear into
them, so, like a pair of redheaded ghouls, we hinted that

black candles, plasticine clay used in the modeling class, and a big supply of pins would take care of them. It did—that is, no one squealed, we escaped the chores, and the astrology class felt it had joined in a great personal triumph. One of them even offered to go personally to the headmistress' study when she was at religious instruction and rub out the black mark from the book in which she recorded all the "criminal" activities of her students.

CHAPTER

Distinguished Visitors—And Then Came Pluto

Although my father and grandmother prepared charts for
many notable people, it was never considered a business in
the financial sense; rather, it was a special service for friends.
Not until I came to the United States did I see that psychic
awareness and astrology did, indeed, have high commercial
possibilities. My grandmother would have laughed in anyone's
face if they had offered her money for her services. "How
can one put a price on helping a person?," she used to say. "If I
say five pounds [about fifteen dollars today], is that all a person's life is worth, or is it too little?"

There is no answer to this type of question. The ideas
about finance differ from society to society, just as social,
moral, and religious customs do. We certainly needed money
in our family. A fine house and land still needed keeping up,
although crippling overheads were not a problem since the
house was paid for and we lived off the land. Surplus stock

was sold off in the proper seasons; horses and dogs were raised, and they in turn yielded an income. At least we were not harassed with monthly bills, for we lived within our means. We ate a variety of foods that would be considered luxurious even in the United States today. Everything was seasonable: salmon fishing came into season on my birthday in late February; abundant fruits and vegetables came in the spring and summer; and with good management, the greenhouses yielded crops all through the year. In the fall, we could eat game birds, such as pheasants; in the winter, venison. The farmyard was always filled with cows to give us milk, cream cheese, and butter, and ducks, geese, chickens, and turkeys were in abundance. The constant stream of visitors always passing through the house provided a ready market for the surplus animals and crops.

There was little waste of food in the house under Grandmother's eagle eye, and enough women were around to make good use of the abundant fruits and vegetables in season. Jams, preserves, sauces, pickles, and bottled fruits were always available. We all developed squirrel complexes, hoarding the special foods that appealed to us.

Today, in the United States, I view the monthly overheads with some horror, noting that they increase each year. Life begins to revolve around making enough money just to keep going, and in a less affluent state of living than I was used to as a child. If Grandmother were born into an incarnation in America today, she might have to charge for her myriad of services to other people—although somehow I doubt she would. I think she might understand why I charge for preparing astrological charts, but never would she condone charging for psychic advice. Not even the rising cost of living could have justified this to her. I used to feel embarrassed at charging for charts, but now I do not; they are time-consuming if they are done properly, and as a woman who earns a living mainly by writing, I know that every minute spent away from the typewriter debilitates my income. I can still be tempted to do free charts for friends, but this is against the advice of my children, who have joined together to take better care of the Leek finances than their mother does. I have always been an easy touch for personal loans and people visiting the house, but this is no longer possible. I think it behooves every psychic and astrologer to literally put his own house in sound financial order so that the basic things in life are taken care of.

I love to have friends around me—again, this is a carry-over from childhood days, when just about everyone in the world seemed to visit us. Those visitors were an extra education for me; I think I have profited by knowing them, even though I was just an inquisitive child when they came. Thomas Hardy, the famous writer and poet, lived in the adjoining county of Dorset. Americans know his work well, including *Jude the Obscure, Tess of the D'Urbervilles,* and *Far from the Madding Crowd,* but how many ever heard Thomas Hardy quietly reading his own poetry as my father cut roses for him to take home?

The exciting Sitwells would come by whenever they were in the area. Sacheverell Sitwell was frighteningly sardonic and unpredictable, and had a macabre interest in psychic phenomena—one moment he would be there, and then he seemed to vanish in thin air. Osbert was robust, blustering, and eager to pick an argument, and Dame Edith was living out her second period of the Renaissance, and had a vitriolic tongue that belied the fragility of her body. All were eccentric, conscious of their own egos, and sometimes dramatized the simple things of life until I thought I was watching a play. Grandmother vied with Dame Edith, deliberately provoking her so that she could enjoy the full flavor of her acid wit, telling her she placed too much store in how she paraded before the world in her remarkable clothes. Because I adored Dame Edith myself, I was a bit surprised at Grandmother standing up to her, but as I grew older, I learned that this was one of the old lady's tactics—to make the person expose something that no one else knew about them. Dame Edith always rose to the bait, and the verbal battles were something to witness.

"She was scrawny when she was young, and she'll be scrawny till she dies," said Grandmother. "She wants her horoscope done, but she lies about her age."

In retrospect, I think Dame Edith was nice to me when I was a child as part of a game of one-upmanship with Grandmother. She was never kind or warm, like so many other people we knew, but I have never lost my admiration for this woman who was uniquely talented and willing to defy conventions in an age when women were supposed to be either pretty playthings or complete academics with little regard for their own appearance. Dame Edith Sitwell certainly cared about her appearance, and she commanded the admiration of the literary world. She always seemed to be unhappy and seemed to reject warmth from others. She received respect and courtesy from my entire family, especially my father—they would spend hours talking about Shakespeare—but she needed Grandmother to whip her verbally. Now I think that she had masochistic tendencies in her nature that had never been acted out. Grandmother knew this was her weak point, so perhaps Grandmother felt that she was filling some vital and mysterious need in the lady's life.

One thing I could be sure about when Dame Edith came—she would announce that she was not going to stay and then linger on, if only to complain that the champagne was not as good as the champagne she usually drank. She was inordinately fond of fresh strawberries; years later, when she was in

London, we would send her some of our first crop. After announcing that she was paying a quick visit, she would "hope that Grandmother was not at home," and then go out of her way to seek her out. The conversation would always get around to her real date of birth, and Grandmother would aggravate her by suggesting dates that were at least ten years earlier than Dame Edith's birthday could possibly have been.

I know that Osbert Sitwell was born in 1892, and his brother Sacheverell in 1897, but Edith was older than her two famous brothers. I suspect that she was born before 1887, which some books give as her date of birth. She hated birthdays and would invent ones that ranged from Gemini through Libra so that complete confusion prevailed whenever we tried to do her horoscope. Edith loved to encourage Grandmother to waste time and then say she had made a mistake. I was always a silent witness.

Edith ruled her brothers with an iron hand, and although both my Grandmother and I tried, it was no use attempting to verify dates with them. Many years later, when I was visiting England, I heard that Dame Edith was very sick and likely to die. With a friend in the acting profession, I visited her. She was intensely frail, but still regal. She insisted that we visit her again, but instead of flowers, we were to bring a bottle of champagne and strawberries. As usual, it was a royal command, and she was still being perverse because neither my friend or I had much money and strawberries were out of season. However, we found some strawberries, borrowed a bottle of champagne from Vivien Leigh, and we smuggled them into her room.

Her tiny hands were dwarfed by enormous rings, which she loved. The jewelry clanked tremulously on the champagne glasses, and she insisted that we drink a toast to her birthday. Perhaps she was telling the truth for once, but I think she was determined to fool me right to the end. She asked about my Grandmother, who had just died, and then she shrank into the big bed and seemed a very tired old lady.

Not even death could daunt a Sitwell though, and as we said good-bye to her, she remarked, "Your Grandmother always talked about reincarnation. I suppose we shall meet again very soon." I left feeling very sad and incongruously clutching an empty champagne bottle in my large handbag. We had to remove the signs of our crime from her guardian. I do hope the two great old ladies, my grandmother and Edith Sitwell, caught up with each other in the afterworld.

Another visitor we had was Thomas Edward Lawrence, who became famous as Lawrence of Arabia. He was born on August 15, 1886, with the Sun in Leo. Actually, he was a most untypical Leo. He ultimately became a leader in the desert, of course, but he was always a nervous wreck when he came to us. My father seemed to get along very well with him, but neither Grandmother nor I really cared for him. Child that I was, I was too young to appreciate his claim to fame, and I really despised him. He certainly did not care for children or dogs, which was an immediate strike against him as far as I was concerned.

Roger, our spaniel, endured him and condescended to ignore him when a member of the family was around. But if Lawrence arrived unexpectedly and Roger saw him come up the driveway, he would immediately go into a frenzy of barking, quite contrary to his usual phlegmatic nature.

The success of his *Seven Pillars of Wisdom*, published in 1926, impressed the whole world. My father was high in its praises, but Grandmother said he had no depth to his nature, so how could he write a good book? She was only sympathetic to his changing his name, first to Shaw, then to Ross. Whatever the truth may be about his personal reasons for doing this, she saw it as a means to finding his right identity.

Grandmother saw Lawrence astrologically as a "child of doom," and she knew that he would come to a bitter end. (As the world knows, he was killed in a cycle accident not far from our home.) Although she disliked him, she was kind to him, and always added a compassionate "poor thing" to his name whenever we talked about him.

I used to keep out of the way when he was around, mainly because I had to restrain Roger, who was likely to sit by the door of the room he was in and howl. Strangely, of all the guests who came to us, I never remember seeing Lawrence smile or laugh, though his voice would vary a great deal in timber; sometimes he was very excitable and virtually unintelligible, while at other times he would talk in a low voice that one could scarcely hear. He was a frustrating visitor from my point of view. I tried to talk to him, but I always drew a blank. Nothing within my world seemed to interest him. I could drag others off to see the latest litter of rabbits or puppies, or show my progress with astrology, but T. E. Lawrence was immune to the wiles of a small imprudent girl, who always had a large shaggy dog following her around.

I have no doubt that Lawrence liked my father, for within Father was all the compassion and humility of a truly great being. I know he helped Lawrence in many ways, chiefly by being there and not being critical. He was never too busy to talk to Lawrence when he arrived unexpectedly, often disheveled, wild-eyed, and unsmiling. As I said, Lawrence always seemed to be on the verge of a nervous breakdown; once I saw him crying in the garden while my father stood by, trying to give one of his beloved plants a lot of concentrated attention. I blurted this out to Grandmother almost before I thought about it. But instead of seeing his fears as a sign of weakness, as I expected her to do, she simply said, "Poor thing, what a karma he has to work out in this life. It would be better if he got it all over and had the chance to start again."

My father was very upset at Lawrence's death in 1935, but I think Grandmother and I were relieved. Maybe this was his chance to start all over again. Today I can admire his literary works and certainly can evaluate them better, but in my mind I shall always remember the T. E. Lawrence stripped of mystique and legends, crying like a child in our garden. My father never mentioned it, although I frequently questioned him about it when I was older. His reply was always enigmatic. "It's not a weakness to know what you are," he said. "In fact, it's a form of strength to know it and have to live in it, especially once you become a celebrity."

I probably learned nothing at all from knowing T. E. Lawrence, although I made up for this by knowing H. G. Wells.

He was my gentle giant, my natural avuncular friend who understood everything. He had all the patience in the world and time enough to spend on his young friend. He was born on September 21, 1866, with the Sun in Virgo, and I know now how important all Virgos are for me. I always get along well with Virgos; indeed, all the men in my family have either the Sun in Virgo, a Virgo Ascendant, or the Moon in Virgo. My two sons are both double Virgos—that is, they have both the Sun and the Moon in this sign. People always wonder at our good relationship, but it is not hard for me to understand when I look at our joint horoscopes.

Small wonder that I adored H. G. Wells, even though I was a tiny child. I wish he was still around in the material form, but I swear he is nearest to me when I am with the many friends I have made recently at the Space Center at Cape Kennedy in Florida.

I haunted Wells when he was around. In those days, I never knew that he was already famous and was ending the last decade of his remarkable life. He knew so much about the stars, psychic phenomena, and space travel that I was convinced he was next to the Supreme Being in his ultimate wisdom. Grandmother loved him too, although space travel was a bit beyond her comprehension. She linked it with astral travel—the freedom of the spirit to release itself from the body and travel on its own—and knew all about man needing to have no limit to his horizons, his mind, and his spirit. Grandmother said his horoscope was fantastic, and he would be the man most remembered as we moved into the Age of Aquarius. I think she was right, but no matter what his fame is to be in the future, I loved him nearly as much as my father.

It was H. G. Wells who took me to see my first eclipse. We had to get up in the middle of the night and walk many miles to see it. I was too small to walk such a distance, so my father and Wells took turns carrying me.

All eclipses are important to an astrologer, as I have since learned, but this one was especially important to me. Eclipses are omens of what can be expected in world events, and the upcoming action is prefigured according to the sign in which the eclipse occurs. When a reporter from *Time* magazine called me in March 1970 about the solar eclipse that drew the attention of the world press to Mexico, he wanted to know what this eclipse meant to me. Well, it meant an earthquake in Turkey and a worldwide health problem. As we know now, we had the earthquake, and we also had typhoid breaking out at a time when we thought such a thing was well under control by advances made by medicine since the turn of the century.

I never study an eclipse in astrology without thinking of H. G. Wells; my one regret is that I was not old enough to truly appreciate him. He was eighty when he died in 1946, and it was too soon. How he would have enjoyed the space program and the launching of the astronauts who set foot on the Moon. With the wisdom and foresight he had in his lifetime, I doubt that he needs to be reincarnated quickly, but if he has indeed been reincarnated, I hope I catch up with the spirit of H. G. Wells once again in my lifetime. The dearest of gentle giants—how we need men like him today, men of foresight and vision who can conceive the future as it will be and are not afraid to be pioneers in thought and action, even if the world may not be ready for them. To be academically brilliant, to know the respect of the literary world, and still to have time for a small child, is remarkable. To me, he was the epitome of manhood and achievement. I think Grandmother respected H. G. Wells more than anyone else who visited us, although she had a strange regard for Alister Crowley, too. And I think Alister Crowley was really in love with her; certainly he respected her, because he was mad about astrology. My father thought he was slipshod, but Grandmother thought he might make it if he practiced more. She could always beat him in a quick assessment of a chart, and he took it in better humor than he did most things. He loved to be thought superior in mental activities as much as he loved to boast of his sexual conquests. No one ever hushed him or said, "Not before the child," so my small pink ears were full of his conversations with Grandmother. Contrary to popular opinion, Crowley did not talk lasciviously about sex, at least not in front of me, but neither did he put any false values on it. It was a tool to be used in life, just as astrology was. "Old lady," he would say, although Grandmother was probably younger than he was, "you teach this child all you can. Sex is in the world, and she'd better know about it; astrology is in the world, and she'd better know about that. And maybe you could teach her some simple forms of magic."

That usually pricked my grandmother into action; she would come back at him about those "simple forms of magic," and they would verbally chase each other with formulas in a game of cat-and-mouse.

Crowley's form of astrology was too mystical for my father, who preferred an academic and purely scientific method. Grandmother resented the idea that an astrologer had to be psychic, although she would grudgingly admit that psychic ability really matters in most things—so why not add a dash of it to astrology? Both she and Father agreed that astrology had to be put into simple forms and intelligible language, but Crowley disagreed. He certainly evolved a strange form of astrology—valid, but practically unintelligible, even to expert astrologers. He loved the tarot cards, too, and he linked them to astrology of course, which is proper, but can cause some confusion for run-of-the-mill astrology students. To this day, I am not quite sure which one of the three of them was completely right, if any of them were right. Perhaps astrology will ultimately reveal many more links with the Old Religion, tarot, Egyptian gods, and Hindu deities. Perhaps when Atlantis is finally discovered again we shall have the answer to so many scientific and esoteric mysteries. Man may need to fall back on the accumulation of ancient wisdom if he is to survive in the Aquarian Age.

Sir James Jeans, the well-known astronomer and scientist, was also a visitor to the house. He was interested not only in astrology, but in psychic phenomena. I have never known two people as excited as he and my father were when Pluto, the dark mysterious planet, was discovered in 1930. Grandmother took it much more phlegmatically, saying that rediscovering Pluto was fine, but what about the other two planets that had to be discovered before we hit the Age of Aquarius?

The prediction that there existed a trans-Neptunian planet

was based on the disturbances in the paths of the known planets. Because of its influence on Uranus, the existence of Neptune had been predicted by Adams and Leverrier; it was discovered by Galle on September 23, 1846, only two full moons distant in latitude from the calculated point of Uranus in the heavens. Leverrier had expressed an opinion that a discovery similar to his would follow. The occurrence of deviations in the paths of the theoretic orbits of Neptune supported the explanation that one or more trans-Neptunian planets might be in existence. Percy Lowell and several other astronomers had started investigations into this possibility, and their first results were published in 1915. Lowell thought the best hypothesis was that the trans-Neptunian planet would be in the heliocentric longitude of 84 degrees in 1914. This would place it in the eastern part of the Constellation of Taurus. As for the mass of the planet, he calculated it to be 1/50,000th of the mass of the sun.

At first, Pluto was mistaken for a comet because of its eccentric path. The Lowell Observatory at Flagstaff, Arizona, had been searching for Pluto for several years when it was found on January 21, 1930, as an object of the fifteenth magnitude, corresponding to the magnitude and location expected by Lowell.

The heliocentric longitude of 108 degrees in 1930 is also in keeping with Lowell's predictions. One can surmise, therefore, that the disturbances in the path of the outer planets find their explanation in Pluto. As reported in *Science*, VII (1930), page 1,850, Pluto was simply called "Planet X." After publication of the discovery of the planet, an eleven-year-old English girl, Venetia Burney of Oxford, submitted the first proposal of a name for the planet—"Pluto." Her father telegraphed this name to the Lowell Observatory at once, and since this was the first proposal to arrive in Flagstaff, it was accepted.

My father was enchanted by the discovery, and his lifetime notes on the astrological influences of Pluto, kept up to the day of his death, have been invaluable to me in my work as an astrologer. He confided in Sir James Jeans his idea that Pluto would be the planet to affect the life of his own children, and in retrospect, I know that he was right. Sir James Jeans always foresaw a time when extrasensory perception and telepathy would be very acceptable. In retrospect, we know that this has happened, and we can trace its roots back to the discovery of Pluto, and the subsequent astrological research into its influences.

I have most of my father's personal papers, which I have updated, and I hope one day to produce a major book on this strange planet that will play an important part in the remaking of the world. In 1950, astrologers began to realize that the Age of Aquarius was indeed dawning. The effects of Pluto became known: it influences regenerative forces that have their counterpart in major changes of religion, morals, sex, and all standards of living. The birth of the first "Pluto-influenced children" was in 1950. As these children grew up they became known as "flower children" and feeling the Plutonian effects on their natal charts, this generation produced a pronounced effect that was without astrological precedent on the whole of society.

Indeed, the effects of Pluto are intriguing to any scientifically minded astrologer. We know that the original astrological meanings of the "old" planets were taken from the characters of the ancient gods, whose names they bear. So we have Aphrodite or Venus, the goddess of love and the fine arts; Ares or Mars, the god of combat and war. In astrology, the planet Venus becomes the principle of love and art, and Mars becomes the principle of combat and war. Zeus or Jupiter is the lord of the heavens, and Poseidon or Neptune, the lord of the sea. Likewise, Hades or Pluto was the lord of the lower regions of the universe, the underworld of darkness.

It is odd that the young English girl chose the name Pluto; even though some people despise mythology, the celestial bodies were not given their names by chance. *Pluton* is Latin for "the rich one." After the fall of his father, Kronos (now called Saturn), Pluto received the netherworld when the universe was partitioned, and he ruled at the side of Persephone, whom he kidnapped. Pluto's mother was Rhea, who is associated with witchcraft, and he was the brother of Zeus and Poseidon. He was ruler over the deceased, and characteristic of his rule was the darkness and the formless, invisible, shadowy world associated with death. Pluto's dwelling was in the depths, and in mythology Pluto is sometimes called *Aides* or *Aideneos*, meaning "the invisible." An old symbol of this invisibility is the so-called helmet or Hood of Aides, which conforms to the hiding cape in Germanic mythology. The hood is made from the scalp of a dog, and the helmet becomes the symbol of Pluto's rulership over the invisible.

Pluto, who was the antithesis of the god of the Sun, Apollo, at first was the irreconcilable enemy of all new life, against which he constantly sent death and destruction. It sounds grim enough in mythology, but today we know that the planet Pluto has many of these traits, which affect people born after 1930. Sacred to Pluto were the narcissus and the cypress, as well as maidenhair. Black sheep were sacrificed to him, and we can find cultural areas of life today in which these customs are reflected. The narcissus is not only a flower, but also the symbol of a life associated with homosexuality. The cypress surrounds many churchyards, and many young people are attracted to the black arts, in which blood sacrifices are not unknown. Many families find they have a black sheep in the family—when this happens, there is always a strong link with Pluto to be found in the personal horo-scope.

Astrologically, there has always been some controversy about which sign or signs to apply to Pluto. Currently there is a wide belief that Pluto has a natural home in Scorpio, rather than Aries, to which it was originally assigned. No sign is as capable of development as Scorpio. This sign embraces people who have fallen to the lowest depths, as well as the highly advanced and spiritual types. To my mind, the Scorpio type is definitely Plutonian and is able to advance to the pinnacles of success if in good aspects, so that either a genius or an adept becomes evident. Scorpio also represents something of the Mephistophelean type of mind that often seeks destruction and then, surprisingly enough, creates something good. This is typical of the regenerative factor in Pluto; it is the phoenix resurrecting itself from its own ashes.

I can see little justification for placing Pluto as a joint ruler in Aries, for Aries is concerned with birth, with nature awakening in the spring in order to wither away, sleep, and die later in the sign of Scorpio. So if we have Aries the beginning of the first push toward life, and Scorpio as death, then Pluto should be the planet of death. Mythology also provides us with other clues, such as Pluto's role as lord of the underworld and his concern with invisibility, which is linked with secrecy, one of the major traits in all subjects born with the Sun in Scorpio or with a Scorpio Ascendant. There is a saying that Scorpio can rise as high as an eagle, or be as low as the belly of a snake, which indicates the tremendous complexity of the Scorpio-types. The lowly developed Scorpio corresponds to the common undeveloped Pluto-type—the serpent or snake-like type. The higher octave of Scorpio corresponds to the eagle, eager to rise to the greatest heights. Persephone,

Pluto's wife, and the avenging goddess, the Medusa, all have serpents in their hair, and serpents come under the rulership of Scorpio. However, Pluto represents dualism, polarity, and disunion, and all these concepts can be found within Scorpio, but not in Aries.

The German astrologer Glahn was the first to recognize the link of Pluto to Scorpio. Charles Carter, the British astrologer, calls Pluto "the wire-puller behind the scenes," claiming that Pluto is related to union, fecundation, copulation, and the secret of "dying" and "being." Pluto also has a double-facedness, just as we find in Scorpio.

There is already evidence that many people born since 1930 have complex characters, and these people have to cleanse themselves of the lower vibrations and throw out the old Adam. They must try to slay the dragon in their own breast, because only the inner change called the "metanceite" can lead to redemption. Today there is a great movement back toward religion on the part of the young, which I think is typical of Pluto-activated people. We have had both the movement of people seeking God within themselves and the anti-Christ movement; now the two ideas are becoming reconciled in a powerful youthful trend toward religion.

Pluto has just emerged from Cancer, where it was cramped, just as the Crab, the symbolic zodiacal creature, is restricted by its shell and must move in a sideways walk in order to progress. The planet was cramped too at its discovery and did not make most of its dramatic traits felt until it moved into Leo, where it burst out in an explosive form—the results of which we are seeing today as ways of life once held sacred disintegrate and a new attitude toward morals, sex, and religion becomes evident.

Those born with Pluto in Leo will proclaim and bring to light a great deal that has long rested in the subconscious.

(One characteristic of Pluto is the storing up of knowledge that will be revealed at the right time.) Today many people are feeling that there must be a spiritual world in addition to the material world, and they seek a bridge between the two. Meanwhile they are fettered by material wishes and pleasures that they were brought up to consider the only values. If they are to find the bridge between two worlds, they must slowly climb up to the higher Pluto principle, which is in many ways analogous to the double-faced Janus principle. Only he who can see forward and backward at the same time can perceive that everything has two sides. Those who can do this are the ones with real foresight. Again the evolutionary principle of Pluto shines through, a bright beacon that makes people want to leave behind the riots, chaos, and general debacles of the world, and step into something better.

However, very few people today can get their personal glimpse of the future (which is brighter than they think). Once the higher vibration is felt by more people, then we can go beyond wars and death to build a world in which peace is not a dirty word, but a way of life. Meanwhile we can only feel the more dastardly effects of Pluto, who must destroy in order to rebuild and in so doing creates a whole generation of disturbed and confused people.

It is much the same with other planets that are unjustly called "malefics"—Saturn, Uranus and Neptune. We shall see Saturn as the great teacher, not the taskmaster; Uranus as the innovator, in which man's inventions provide more leisure time, and the ability to use that leisure well. Neptune will cease to be the wayward, deceptive planet, and will be attuned to people conscious of the occult forces in their highest form. As the planet of regeneration, Pluto will play a vital role with these planets: the link between the dying Age of Pisces with its pomp, piety, poverty, and poetry, and the great new spiritual Age of Aquarius, in which we shall see less of man's inhumanity to man. First Pluto must grind down and take its sacrifices; then it will do its phoenixlike act of being reborn into a bright new world.

Somehow I think H. G. Wells will be reincarnated to see this a reality. After all, he was probably conscious of it before anyone else was.

CHAPTER 4

Where Have All the Beautiful People Gone?

It is difficult to remember who my very first important client was, but I suspect it was Ian Fleming. He was certainly not world famous when I did his horoscope in the early part of the Second World War, but the potential for fame as a writer was there. Although he was engaged in special duties for the Intelligence Department of the British Armed Forces and reveled in the adventures that came his way, he was always envious of me because I was a writer. I do not mean envious in a vicious sense—Fleming was too sensible for that—but when he thought of writing, his heart seemed to be torn out by frustration. Nothing else would console him—not adventure, nor praise for his courage, nor love affairs, nor worldly possessions.

He always had to live two different lives. Allowing for the fact that to find a typical sign at all in the zodiac is very difficult, he was in many ways a prototype of the typical Gemini.

There is great difficulty when one has the versatile imagination of the twins to battle with. Fleming was whimsical, erratic, alternately brilliant and pathetic, but never dull. His
charm was like the dew on the grass—exposed to too much
light and warmth, it would disappear, and I was surprised at
the toughness of the man beneath the charming surface. He
enjoyed parading his knowledge, but he was also totally secretive and could clam up in the middle of a sentence. He
would always give a listener enough to intrigue him; most
conversations with Ian Fleming were like reading a detective
novel, only to find that someone had removed the important
final chapter. So I had to make up a lot of my own endings.

It was not my affection that appealed to him, but the moments when my redheaded Irish temper came out. We could
duel with fiery words, wounding and jousting, until one of us
would retreat. I never could run away from words, but he
always had some face-saving method of bowing out. I knew
he was dedicated to his intelligence work, and this got him
out of many a vicious verbal match. Once he made me so
mad with barbed jibes and insults that I belted him with the
misunderstood but delectable fish indigenous to the British
breakfast menu—a freshly kippered herring. Instead of being
furious, as I expected him to be, he showed typical Geminian
unpredictability—he laughed and insisted on having the kip-
per cooked so he could eat it.

Most of his romantic affairs were disastrous, but the disasters were usually incurred by the other person, rarely by him.
He hated women who compromised in anything, and I suppose
that is why I survived with him. I was completely arrogant
in my youth, as selfish as he was, and I could never admit I
was wrong; I strode through the world as if I had paid
an option on it. The memory of how I was in those days now
makes me wrinkle my nose with disdain, but it was part of

the trial by fire I had to go through to survive in a world that was not welcoming astrologers with open arms, especially when they were following such an unorthodox religion as witchcraft.

Fleming loathed anything to do with the occult—at least he professed this in public. In private, he was not above questioning me about such things as extrasensory perception and telepathy, and we would argue for hours about the validity of psychic phenomena. Like most skeptics, he could be quite disarming; he admitted that he followed his intuition when he was in difficulties, and he boasted that this intuition got him out of scrapes far more quickly than logic and reason ever did. What a tormented mixture the man was with his two-way mind forever probing. One moment he would be seeking assurance of life after death, and the next he would be saying he had a death wish and was convinced he would only pass this way once.

I pointed out that his success would come late in life and would transfer him from one brilliant career to another, and marriage would be a stepping-stone to success. I saw this come true, and I enjoyed the triumph he had as the creator of James Bond. (It was obvious to me that the James Bond series consisted of fragments of his own life.) No man enjoyed success in his profession more than he did, and the Sun in Gemini was a great asset. He was versatile, voluble, articulate, and literate, and very much a daredevil in his attitude toward life.

I remember that he once told me he preferred a short sweet life to a long, drawn-out old age with the possibility of inaction or immobility. He persistently asked me when he would die, as if he had a desire to get his affairs in order and reach the end of his life. To an astrologer, this is not a desirable question; many schools of thought today believe that people are not able to think coherently about death, so they should not be apprised of the possible year. Of course, it is possible to discover the approximate time of death through astrology, but perhaps an astrologer should be like the doctor who knows that certain illnesses will last a certain time and then death will be inevitable, but he withholds this information from the patient. The eighth house of Scorpio can tell an astrologer a great deal, but personal charts have to be progressed and many factors, such as possible eclipses, must be taken into consideration.The major characteristics of the sign in which the eclipse appears indicates the areas likely to be affected by the eclipse. For instance, an eclipse in Virgo, such as we had in 1970, indicates to an astrologer that major health problems are likely in the world. We know now in retrospect that cholera, once thought to be abated in Europe, broke out there at the time of this eclipse. Astrologers saw this a year before the eclipse happened, but imagine how the world press would have laughed in 1969 at the announcement that cholera would claim thousands of victims in 1970! As all scientific men knew, cholera had not reared its ugly head there for many decades.

Personal death is predicted in a similar fashion, but there are many ramifications within the personal horoscope, so no hard and fast rule can be set down. However, it is necessary to discover the aspects made to the eighth house of the specific horoscope. Ethically, I think it is better to reserve information concerning death, except in very special circumstances, because the philosophy and teachings of most orthodox religions do not prepare people for living with a foreknowledge of this important time of transition from one life to another.

A lawyer once came to visit me. He had the usual aura of secrecy lawyers like to maintain when they come to an astro-

loger. He was concerned in a European case in which a vast
sum of money was involved, and due to the entail laws of
inheritance in force in Europe at the time, it helped him to
know when the death of a very old man would occur. (The
entail laws allow only the eldest son to inherit even without a
will in his favor.) I did indeed find out the time of death, and
it occurred within twenty-three hours of my predicted time. I
presume the lawyer had time to make the necessary arrangements, but I did not ask for any details. He offered me half
of the agreed sum at the time of the prediction, and half "if
and when it happened." As far as I was concerned, that was
no sort of deal, and I ended up not delivering the horoscope
until he had paid me in full. Finally he paid me a good fee. I
even felt a sense of victory; I beat the law at its own game by
forcing him to pay up on the barrelhead before any work was
done.

In the case of Ian Fleming, we managed to compromise on
the question of his death without spoiling our friendship.
Without telling him the exact date, I explained that he need
not expect a long drawn-out illness; death would come quickly, and it certainly did. He had a couple of preliminary warnings in the form of heart attacks. Then he died very suddenly,
with just enough time to murmur to the ambulance atten-
dants, "It was quite a lark," which just about summed up his
remarkable life.

Ian Fleming made a great impression on me; he stirred up
some strange and contradictory emotions. I admired so much
about him yet disliked as much, but we managed to have a
good friendship that had advantages for both of us. I really
believe I understood him, as much as anyone can understand
a man who lived and died an enigma. Astrology helped in
this; his mercurial temperament might have destroyed our
friendship if I had not been able to evaluate him through his

horoscope and know the basic frustrations of his dual image.

It was many years before I met up again with a volatile character expressing the best and worst of the Gemini traits. Many, many years later, when I was in New York, I met my first American editor—a woman this time, but as we grew to understand each other, I was astonished at how she echoed the Ian Fleming image of versatility. However, she did not have the pioneering, adventurous nature in the same way that he had. Instead, it manifested itself in her willingness to take on controversial authors and flaunt them to the public as her personal discoveries. I know that she must have fought hard to get me accepted by the conservative publishing house she represented, but she did it, and she launched me in a way that still has me marvelling at the breakthrough at a time when witchcraft and astrology were less acceptable as commercial publishing ventures.

Naturally I did the horoscope of my first editor in the United States, and it was remarkably good. She was interested in psychic phenomena because she saw that it had sales potential, but she was wary of astrology. Talking to her about it was like trying to explain a symphony to a deaf man. But, like all Gemini ruled by the planet Mercury, she loved logic. The only thing to do was to prove to her that astrology works on an individual level. I carefully prepared her natal chart and a series of progressed ones, and I produced just enough salty details of her past life to titillate her insatiable curiosity. Four houses are concerned with finance: the second house generally shows all gains made from personal efforts; the fifth, gains through children, pleasurable occupations, speculation, and enterprises; and the eleventh house, gains through friends or profession. The eighth house is the one that shows gains through partners or legacies. My good editor's horoscope showed that her eighth house was of considerable interest: it showed a relation dying, and her financial status would be increased by a legacy. After the aunt died and left her the legacy she never argued strongly against astrology.

Today she is with another company. We rarely meet, and our friendship consists of long phone calls. Sometimes we scream at each other, for I frequently feel that authors are exploited in America. They have to go out and sell their books to the American public via promotions, numerous TV and radio shows, and travel thousands of miles, when they should be sitting at the typewriter. She can never keep an appointment either, which makes me furious, for I am a stickler for time. But she has all the purring charm of a Gemini and is a wizard at putting a book together. Most of the suggestions she makes are very valid, so I have learned to follow her advice instead of arguing. I should have learned this lesson long ago when I knew Ian Fleming, but many years had to be added to my life to get me away from being an arrogant, impossible young person, who had had too much too quickly.

When she feels that things are in a state of flux in her hectic life, she calls me to get a reading. Like most Geminis, her sense of timing is not too good, so she generally calls when I am up to my ears in getting a new book out and demands an instant rundown on herself. Her horoscope is practically tattooed on my brain, and I do a quick check on her at the beginning of every month.

Always conscious of their basic charm, intellectual Geminis can generally get away with anything. It is not unusual for them to ride roughshod over people, even if they like them. Ian Fleming gave me a good experience in dealing with other members of his sign, and today I stand up and yell to outdo them if I have to. One beautiful thing is that few

Geminis are ever resentful or seek revenge; they may have a
short fuse to their temper and may be utterly inconsiderate,
but they are so adaptable that reconciliation comes easily to
them, and they never bear grudges. I think they always keep
an ace in the hole—they are sure they will be right the next
time, and they work on a law of compensating averages.

Our family used to spend most winters in the south of
France, migrating like swallows at the first hint of the cold,
damp English winter. It was part of the seasonable activities
for many Britishers, and we all looked forward to the villa in
Nice or Mentone. The deliciously equable climate of the
French Riviera must surely make it one of the best places in
the world to live. As I grew older, the time spent there grew
longer, but generally we left England just before Christmas
and stayed in France until the end of April or the beginning
of May.

The south of France was a great place for astrologers, and
my family was very well known among residents and fellow
migrants. My father was happy to meet old friends, including
engineers from Germany and Spain, and I was always glad to
have a chance to explore. As usual, I was a show-off. Every
year brought me more knowledge of astrology, and many of
the embassies in Nice and Mentone invited us to parties. I had
the stamina, since I was a nondrinker and a nonsmoker, to go
to as many as thirty parties a week. It sounds impossible
now, but the French are fond of luncheon parties, so I had to
go to all of those. The immigrant and White Russian refugees
loved to have dinner parties and soirees, and they too were a
must. There was little time for relaxing on the beach.

In the south of France, I first began to earn money for
making up charts, and I did so with a sense of guilt. My
father indulgently regarded this as pocket money but Grandmother even eyed with disdain a present I accepted for her.
After a few firm talks with her, she grew out of this attitude,

and I was thankful, for I do not think I could have borne her silence on the subject for too long. I had to suffer a few sarcastic remarks, though, such as "Why not go to Brighton Pier?" (This was the local resort; it had been elegant in Regency days, but it was gradually becoming the center for all that was way-out and avant-garde.) Fortunately, I had a tough skin against these remarks, but one season I nearly wore myself out with séances, and I learned my lesson. I chalked it up as a necessary experience, which it certainly was. I never knew so many people who were totally obsessed with sitting in the dark around a table, expecting that Aunt Mildred would bother to come through to them.

Because of my youth, I enjoyed the shocks that happened at the séance table—cold rushes of air on hot nights, eerie noises, and lights that went on and off with no human hand flicking the switches. But I knew this way of life was not for me: séances are easy enough, but something in my nature craved a better way to spend the evenings than receiving nebulous messages from other people's dead relations.

Astrology, though, was different. I now knew enough to avoid doing something that I warn my own students against doing today, that is, whipping out the "instant horoscopes" and giving quick rundowns of character and predictions. Gradually I learned to be discriminating, and I built up an exclusive clientele who looked forward to my yearly visit. I earned more money, kept my self-respect, and laid the foundation for many friendships and a much more meaningful way of life. Many people in the south of France came to me incognito; some came fearfully, and some arrogantly; others were genuinely interested in knowing about the planetary trends. The aggressive ones I could afford to ignore because each year predictions I had made through astrology came true and added to my reputation.

Society in the south of France had its special grapevine

that started at teatime in the Jockey Club, went through the casinos, and wafted out on the breeze of the mistral into the salons of the great houses on the hill. France, of course, is a Catholic country, but no one allowed religious scruples to interfere with the avid desire to see what the future held. I was too young then to recognize everyone who came to me, and in the early days many famous people wintered on the Riviera. Titles were as common as the name John in America; foreign dignitaries speaking strange languages were just as likely to come as some of the better known crowned heads of Europe. This was the great period when the Hotel Negresco was the hub of "the cream of society." Balls were fashionable; anyone who had an Order to wear did so, and no one thought they had stepped out of a Friml musical comedy. They were great, glorious, golden days of glittering names, meetings at the horse races, and large yachts. If the old way of society was dying on the vine, it still kept up an appearance and was going to die as hectically and gloriously as it lived.

No one ever mentioned fees, and now that I come to think of it, there were very rare occasions when people actually offered money at the time they collected their horoscopes. What is more remarkable is that no one reneged on some form of payment, ranging from gifts in kind to vast amounts of foreign currency, sometimes gold sovereigns, which I kept, and handfuls of silver that I spent as quickly as it came in. Many exotic presents, the like of which I have never had again, flowed freely into my household. It was good that we traveled on the Blue Train from Nice to Paris and then from Paris to Le Havre, where we boarded the packet steamship back to Southampton, for on a ship the elderly Aga Khan, father of Prince Ali, always gave me massive quantities of caviar and insisted that it had to be eaten with his own special silver spoon. He loved company and always wanted to stay and talk for a long time while his aides tried not to look uneasy or bored. He worried about his family and his country and his obesity, although it must have been a great consolation when he returned to India and was weighed against his weight in precious stones. He was a happy man, vastly interested in astrology, and he liked to compare my European version with Indian astrology. The only special requirement he had—he made a great point about it—was that I must never reveal his horoscope or do the horoscope of his wife. The wealthy and the gracious are inclined to have strange foibles, and it was no hardship to adhere to his wishes.

Sometimes he would send the date and place of birth to me by special messenger, with a request that the horoscope should be delivered to his emissary on a certain date and at the exact time indicated. He was a good client, and again, I was happy to adhere to his wishes. Some of the horoscopes he sent along were interesting, dependent on the sex of the subject. The female ones were mostly concerned with romance, but the males were obviously business acquaintances. At first, I thought he was just checking out ladies who appealed to his romantic nature, but I think he was also taking a great interest in his staff. Like most rulers of nations, especially despotic monarchs, he knew that the head that wears a crown can be very uneasy. Smiling manners are often a facade for political plans designed not so much to remove the crown, but to siphon off some of the power.

The elderly Aga Khan was wily and able to have the best of several worlds at one time. He was quite at home among European society, but was always conscious of his Indian background. His ancestors had always used astrologers, and he was wise enough to know that an unofficial but loyal "friend at court" in the twentieth century could be an astrologer.

Although the Aga Khan never wanted me to do his wife's horoscope, he was vastly interested in the horoscopes of his children, especially that of the son who finally succeeded him. The fourth Karim Aga Khan was born on December 13, 1936, with his Sun in Sagittarius. His romantic interludes became an integral part of the social columns throughout the world, but the father was not merely interested in his son's love life. "Tell me what he is really like," he would say. "How will he be received by my people, and how good will he be as a leader of men?"

Unfortunately, there was little to tell, because there were no signs that the son would ever earn the respect of his people in the way his father hoped he would. He had an afflicted Jupiter that accounted for some of the seasons of discontent that are forever manifesting themselves in his life. He has been compelled to seek more and more wealth, for the richness of his inheritance was never enough for him. I suppose this accounted for his constant search for an ideal woman. Then, when he thought he had found her, as he may have done in Rita Hayworth, he was never to be quite sure, so the search had to continue.

We had many, many consultations about his horoscope. The kindly old ruler, grandfather of Prince Karim and now the ruling Aga Khan, paid the rent on my house for the season, and sent more caviar than ever before, so I suppose he felt I did my work well. The gentleman loved European society, and I think he was very happy when he was living on the Riviera.

My great aunt raised Pekingese dogs in her villa at Mentone, and although the Aga Khan was not what I consider a great

animal lover by British standards, he would frequently
ask which puppies we had for sale. He never wanted
to choose one himself, so he left such choices to me. When I
had described a particular puppy to him, he would follow up
the conversation by sending me an address to which I had to
deliver the puppy at a specific time of the day. He had a special liking for "fawn ones with very black faces," and one
season I think I helped to populate the entire Riviera with
dogs from Heathcliffe kennels.

This was a pleasant and profitable sideline, for we received
thousands of dollars for such stock. We had kennels in England, and our main sire was a famous Alderbourne-bred stud
dog called Alderbourne Tuantoo, although he was later aug-
mented by a glorious dog called Kyratown Marvelus of
Heathcliffe. This dog represented a considerable financial
investment on my part. I actually purchased him after a tip
from the Aga Khan to back a racehorse that won at good
odds. I used to bet on horses a great deal as a result of knowing the Indian ruler, and I met many of his friends who were
racehorse owners or devotees of The Sport of Kings.

When I went over the Channel for my winter vacation, I
generally took several Pekingese to augment my great aunt's
Maria-Fedora Riviera kennel. I think we were the first people
in the world to consistently breed whole litters of pure white
Pekingese dogs that retained their snowy whiteness in adult
life. Once the Aga Khan knew we had a new strain, he
changed his order for dogs from "fawn with black faces" to
"pure white, and be certain there is not a dark hair anywhere." He was intrigued that we called the principal stud
dog Winston Churchill, and he asked me to name a puppy
after him. He also made some outrageous suggestions for the
names of a litter of female puppies, but by this time I was
used to his sense of humor. His interests were varied, and he

was very unpredictable in his requests which ranged from horoscopes of people he could not stand to those he obviously adored, and with requests for puppies thrown in for good measure. The Aga Khan liked every puppy to have the best possible pedigree, and he was very impressed by a list of champions appearing in the pedigree. I calculated that he only gave the puppies to people whose horoscopes I considered pleasant ones, for which I was thankful. After the war, I went back to the south of France as the youngest judge ever to officiate at a championship show, and I also had the honor of showing dogs that became triple champions. To be a triple champion, the dog had to win in three different countries, which was no small achievement. I generally did the circuit of France, Switzerland, and Germany with considerable success.

Years later I became one of the first people to realize the potential of doing horoscopes for dogs, and I called them my dogiscopes. After all, every living thing has a relationship to the planetary influences, and after breeding pedigree dogs and acting as midwife for many Pekingese mothers, I was always able to get the time of birth right. I did not waste time showing dogs that had no hope of winning in the show-ring.

The late Queen Marie of Romania was interested in astrology, but was fearful of anyone knowing it. This I found remarkable. She was a strong, individualistic type, and astrology was so fashionable on the Riviera that she could not have been afraid of public opinion. She was not financially generous, probably because of her own depleted circumstances. Later I found she often got paid for making public appearances, and this must have galled her proud nature. She was gracious enough, but always liked to talk about people in the same social set. Sometimes I think she came to me simply to see if she was missing anything on the local grapevine, but

I learned discretion very early in life, and I never gossiped about another person's horoscope or discussed any business, love, or sex life with anyone but the subject of the horoscope. At that time I was too closely involved with my clients. Now that so many are dead, it is not so indiscreet to mention them.

Men were much more generous than women, but I had no complaints about the gifts and money that literally rolled in every day. One of my most awkward gifts was a baby ocelot, which I dearly loved. I was staying with my aunt, who kept up to twenty Pekingese dogs, and a baby ocelot was a handful there. In order to restore peace at Villa la Rosèe, I reluctantly tried to sell the ocelot, but there were no takers until I found a lonely man living in the hills. He did not have any money, but I could see that the ocelot would have a good home, and the two were made for each other. Resigned to giving the ocelot away, I went into the Cafe L'Oasis, my favorite lunchtime haunt. My usual Piscean optimism and good fortune prevailed. My lonely friend in the hills had quite a cache of jewelry, and as I was used to buying and selling jewelry as a sideline whenever I was on the Riviera, I finally managed to sell most of the stuff he had and gain quite a good commission for myself.

With the money made on this deal, I followed the advice of an elderly Persian gentleman who frequented the casino and taught me how to "buy money." This was one of my most valuable lessons in my life. I used to go to the currency exchange early in the morning, study the board, and use ESP to anticipate which nation's currency should be bought. If I felt like it—and always with the advice of my strange Persian friend—I would go back in the afternoon and sell the currency for some other form of money, if it yielded a profit. Money, I had learned by now, was a useful commodity, whether it was escudos, francs, marks, dollars, or sterling. Money is a commodity very necessary to one's peace of mind and is a means of changing one's way of life at a whim.

Although I made a small fortune every winter on the Riviera, I also had a happy knack of spending it. Today I am much more careful, but what a lot of pleasure there is in spending money! Often it can do someone else a lot of good, such as going to a small café that is on its last legs and is preparing to fold up. One good party, such as I used to give in Nice or Mentone, put many a debilitated café on its feet again. While I have never been interested in simply amassing money for the sake of storing it in a bank, I have developed a healthy regard for what it can do. However, one must always be the master of money, and never its servant.

Few of those who knew the south of France in its best, opulent days had any concern about money; it came and it went, and so long as the days were happy, no one seemed to care much. Those who had plenty of it were eager to share it with the latest astrologer, and those who did not have it were always welcome, providing they had the right family background, for the Riviera was the last stronghold of a feudal way of life. If you had money, a title, and good manners, you had it made. There were factions of society there who would settle for just one of these attributes, but no one wanted to be known as a social hanger-on or a freeloader. The United States is a democratic country in concept, but it could learn a lot from the pooling of resources that went on among the landed gentry of the great old houses.

The only really mean man I met on the Riviera was the late Somerset Maugham. Although he was born with the Sun just in Aquarius on January 25, 1874, he showed the parsimonious characteristics of Capricorn males. He was respected because of his talent, but he lacked much of the warmth that

so many other people had. Perhaps it is unfair to demand
that writers have a certain ebullience of personality. Maybe I
knew Somerset Maugham in his off-days. I admired his work
and loved his house, but I could never really like the man. He
was patronizing about astrology and thought it was the same
as palm reading.

I took special masochistic delight in doing Maugham's
horoscope and presenting it to him. Later on I worked out
the time he would die and felt no remorse. I used it to prove
a point to my editor, who was at Southern Television Studios, where I worked for some time after the Second World
War. We were able to get Maugham's obituary out well before
anyone else, and somewhat grotesquely, I realized that I
made more money doing an obituary based on his horoscope
than I ever had for doing it when he was alive. He had paid
for his horoscope with a mediocre dinner, and I am allergic to
bad meals, even when the silver is good and the flowers are in
an elegant arrangement.

Filmstars abounded in the south of France, but I did not
know many of them in my capacity as an astrologer. Years
later I met Rita Hayworth when she was married to Karim
Aga Khan, but it was a strange meeting. She was in a car that
he was driving at a fantastic speed when it crashed, and I was
the first on the scene. She screamed hysterically and then
cried enough tears to swell the Mediterranean.

I frequently met the daughters of the Prince of Monaco. I
liked them and vaguely remember feeling sorry for them.
They lived a very restricted, conservative life, hemmed in by
protocol that did not extend itself to their brother, who married Grace Kelly. The children and I went to their wedding,
which was a dreamy, romantic affair in keeping with the
fairy-tale-princess legend. At first glance at her horoscope,
she does not appear to have much in common with her Sun

in Scorpio, but she actually has great depth of character, is intensely secretive (a typical Scorpion trait), and has much more strength of purpose and character than anyone would imagine. I think the fairy-tale princess is quite capable of using an iron hand in a velvet glove in order to keep many events in her private life under control. She is a great friend of one of America's most famous astrologers, Carroll Righter, and recently she held a birthday party for fellow Scorpios, including Pablo Picasso.

Once I had a strange encounter that I had occasion to remember later in life. I was traveling on a train from Paris for a long weekend with a friend from the Louvre who invited me to dig with her at the Roman ruins then being excavated at Avignon. Into our carriage came two military men, and soon we were in deep conversation with them, forgetting the old cautious warning of many an English mother to any daughter traveling alone on the Continent: "Don't speak to strange men in railway carriages." Our traveling companions were army captains; both were very good-looking, but one was especially handsome. He was tall and lean, and he wore his uniform well. His name was Captain De Gaulle.

On the way down, we talked about astrology, palm reading, and séances. He did not have the sparkling nonchalant small talk of his companion, and he seemed to be a sad man. To while away the time and with encouragement from my friend from the Louvre, I did a sketchy thumbnail horoscope of him, but some of the old family intuition took over in the process. I promised to do a full horoscope later on and send it to him. Some strange quirk of intuition made me tell him that had he been born in another age, he would have worn the Crown of France. The country had long been a republic, of course, and we laughed about this. Happily we went on our way, not knowing, except for my intuition, that we had met a man who was to leave his mark on the history not only of his own country but of the world. Avignon was exciting, and soon the memory of the train journey and our traveling companions was forgotten as we scraped away at the earth which in time was to reveal some great relics of the Roman Age.

Then, during the Second World War, I was in the Piccadilly Hotel in London when I saw the same handsome French officer again. He came toward me and greeted me effusively, which was very flattering. He crossed the room with a few strides, gripped my hands, and said, "I seem to be a long way from being King of France, since today I am in exile from my own country."

General De Gaulle was born on November 22, 1890, with his Sun in Sagittarius. My further and more complete investigation of his horoscope showed that he had many Leo characteristics, which gave him an obvious trend toward natural leadership. He could indeed have been a king and was more fitted to it than the Sun-in-Leo characteristics of Napoleon Bonaparte. But they both had many things in common, including a natural tendency to be domineering and despotic in a country that sought to eliminate royalty in its own manner. His horoscope showed that he would return victorious to his own country and fulfill the destiny of greatness shown in his natal horoscope.

I followed his career with interest right through to his death, and when other astrologers predicted he would be assassinated or die two years before he actually did, I could never go along with them. Much in his horoscope had to be fulfilled because he was part of a great political machine, and he was as closely knit with the affairs of his beloved France as his own head was to his body. He was born to achieve greatness, and he was prepared when greatness was thrust upon him. I think his finest moment was when he retired. He left the Presidency with immense dignity, cutting off the phone from his private residence to the statehouse and retiring into the background when he knew his path of destiny was nearly at an end. Even his death was impressive: the man who saw himself as the spirit of France let France come to him at his death. He lived almost classically within the framework of his natal horoscope. He had his critics, who were quick to point out his weaknesses, for they were such that they varied according to the position of the political opinions of the observer into his life. He was the ultimate in nationalists, believing that France was for the French. He was a great character who could make even his most valiant opponent look diminished both in stature and personality by comparison. Born to be a king, he must have known many frustrations when he became President. He was a staunch Catholic, as befits the President of a Catholic country, but in his search for truth he also looked into séances and astrology, taking what he wanted from them and dismissing the rest.

Frequently I look back with nostalgia to those old days on the Riviera, but I take some consolation in knowing I was involved in that beautiful part of the world in the early days of my life in astrology. Life was always good on the Riviera, until about ten years ago. I wish I could still live there, but President De Gaulle made it increasingly difficult for foreigners to live there due to high taxation; nor can I settle for the tourist-type place that it has now become. I never left the world of glamor, but merely changed the setting. As I went about my business as an astrologer, I also had to come to grips with living. I took time to gaze upward at the heavens and know that man, in his smallness of stature, has a link with the celestial bodies millions of miles away.

CHAPTER

War Years—The Eclipse of Pleasure

The advent of the Second World War curtailed the winter sessions in the south of France, and residents in Britain settled down to a life of cold austerity. Our family was fortunate to live in the country, where we could grow food, for strict rationing of a type that is incomprehensible to anyone of this generation was enforced. How people in the cities survived is beyond understanding. Take one ounce of butter sometime and wonder how you can possibly make it last a week—but somehow, people managed. Most of all, they kept cheerful despite horrifying bomb raids that culminated in the invention of the doodle-bug bomb by Wernher von Braun, then in charge of missiles in Germany and now a big wheel in the United States space industry. The doodle-bug bombs were cruel and killed more civilians than military men, but I suppose everyone in Great Britain was really a part of the Armed Forces. Women worked long, hard hours in armament factories, and men beyond military age banded themselves together in surveillance groups called the Civil Defense. Many of these older men died as they guarded their communities in the face of fires and terrible bomb damage.

The Second World War was not fought on military battlefields, but along the winding lanes of the country; it touched every aspect of life. No one was safe, whether in uniform or not. I remember helping to dig deep trenches on the grounds around our house. We had to make expeditions to the seashore to drag back thousands of pounds of sand, which all the youngsters in the house grimly packed into burlap bags. These were placed along the sides of the trench, which we had to use frequently because we were not too far away from the port of Southampton, which was used as an exit point for many troops. When we lay in the shelter looking up to the skies, astrology seemed a distant subject as the fireworks of exploding bombs dominated the night sky, their brilliance putting the stars to shame.

Glamorous visitors to the house were few and far between. Instead, we had a motley assortment of strangers, many of them refugees from the cities, and most of them children, aged, or infirm. We had various relations and friends who managed to escape from Germany, leaving everything behind them. I remember standing on the shores of the English Channel at the time of Dunkirk, hearing the big guns blazing away, and the sand beneath my feet was trembling as if an earthquake might break loose. We lived in a landscape of barbed wire, cement towers, khaki uniforms or the navy blue of the Royal Navy, and in a climate of fear; tomorrow might bring the end of our world. A way of life died all around us as communications were cut off with the Continent and with our exotic friends of the golden Riviera days. There were very few men left in our village, since most of them entered the service at once. Then it seemed the right and proper thing to do, because we all seemed to know that this was ultimately a war for personal survival. Today the United States is at war in a foreign country, but there is a big difference in how a person feels when the enemy is the width of the English Channel away, just twenty miles. War on one's own doorstep is like finding a burglar in the house.

I am fanatically against the war in Vietnam because no one can ever tell me what it is all about. I think a lot of other people feel the same way: it is too obtuse, too distant, to make an impact on everyday life in the United States, as the war in Europe did. I do not mean any disrespect to families who have lost a son in the current war; I grieve with them, but I can also understand a generation that revolts against this mysterious war. I do not believe, however, that any young man in the United States would refuse to put up a fight if the enemy were in his own country, for the instincts to survive are basic to everyone.

We fought because we had to survive, not just because someone issued a decree in Parliament. I joined the sixtieth section of the London Red Cross, which was supposed to be an elegant group of young society women and had the distinction of being the only section that allowed its members to wear brass buttons on the uniform. This honor had been won in a campaign on the field in the First World War when the sixtieth section covered itself with honor and glory. We had a big tradition to live up to, and after a few days of training in the Medical Corps, we ceased to be "young society ladies." One good bombing in London during the blackout united us as a hard-working team. We ditched our civilian clothes and said good-bye to parties. People like my roommate, Elizabeth Bowes-Lyon, a cousin of the Queen, contributed her debutante's tiara to the war effort.

I became a nurse in the famous military hospital at Netley, near Southampton. Originally, when Great Britain had an empire in India, an architect was asked to design two large military hospitals, one for India and one for Britain. Apparently the architect's plans got crossed; Netley found itself with a huge military hospital that was suitable for a torrid climate and had a definite Indian motif about it. I ended up in the Netley Hospital's Prisoner of War Department because I spoke French well and knew a smattering of German. It was a nerve-racking experience, dealing with prisoners of war who were sick, many of whom had lost a limb. The Germans were aggressive and rude to all the female staff. They were not truly interested in living, and many fought against medical attention. It was a great lesson in discipline to nurse the enemy and know he was still the enemy. We were told that we must not, under any circumstances, allow a prisoner to provoke us. In theory, it was fine; in practice, very hard. We were all high-spirited girls from good families, and every one of us had men from the family in the service. We had to withstand barrages of abuse, physical onslaught, and sexual advances, and we still had to try to be pleasant.

One day I heard that my cousin Edwin's plane had been shot down in Germany. The telegram said he was "missing and presumed lost in battle combat." I entered the ward, which was at the top of the building, and was hit full in the chest by a large bouquet of flowers still in its bowl—it was a painful experience. I became blazing mad; I stalked over to the patient, and slapped his face on both sides. Many years later, when I saw the film *Patton*, I knew exactly the type of demon that got into the General when he slapped an American soldier. Of course, I was reprimanded and confined to barracks for a week. The soldier was moved to another hospital, which showed tact on the part of the Commanding Officer. All the girls felt that the slap was administered on behalf of all of us, for we had had a particularly nerve-racking week. I was working on night duty at the time, but we had so many casualties that there was no distinct changeover for any of us.

We stayed until an entire hospital ship checked into the hospital; the operating theaters were working like mad. I used to leave the theater dazed, physically and mentally sick, wondering when it would all end. On duty in the wards, when we were alerted that a wave of bombers was coming over, we always had to check the blackouts. Not a single window could be undraped. Many of the prisoners of war who could walk would cheer when there was a raid and would sing German songs as they tried to tear down the blackout coverings. We had to fight them off and sometimes threaten them. The German soldier was inclined to despise the female in uniform, but I learned I could scream as loud as he could, and I picked up enough swear words to start a new dictionary.

The sixtieth section of the London Red Cross may have started out in Netley as a group of young society ladies, but after a few months of campaigning like this, we had forgotten what the word "lady" meant. We were hardened Boadiceas, ready to be in the thick of battle twenty-four hours a day. We all came from families that frowned on girls drinking and smoking, but we learned both from the male members of the 101st Bridging Company of the Royal Engineers. We all had officers' privileges, which included using officers' messrooms when we had time. We ate fairly well, but the elegant sixtieth section was given sleeping quarters in barracks that had once been condemned as unfit for use by British soldiers. We thrived on hard conditions, hard palliasses, rough army blankets, and no sheets, because they were needed in the hospital, where supplies of everything dwindled as the war progressed.

I was with the group of nurses who survived Anzio Beach,

a grim nightmare in which I saw my dear friend, Captain
de Lisle, killed in a particularly nasty way by being blown to
pieces. Then it was up to the Hebrides, a wild deserted lot of
islands off the north coast of Scotland, with six nurses, two
doctors, and three hundred sick men on an island two miles
wide and six long. The winds blew so strongly that to go outside the barracks we had to hold rope handrails in order to
stand upright, much less walk. Sweeping gulls screamed day
and night. This area was constantly under fire because Great
Britain's warships were nearby, and the Germans wanted to
kill the convoy system that protected much of the shipping.
There were a few people living on the island, who were bewildered by the war and loathed the flux of military people
that drew attention to their tiny homes. After a while,
though, the natives grew to like us. They were dear Gaelic
people who had little themselves, but were content to share
the meager produce of their farms. We lived on roughly
cooked "bannocks," a form of rounded homemade bread
something like a bun, but much harder, and on eggs—seagull
eggs, plover eggs, anything with a shell on it. The healthy air
whipped our youthful, robust appetites to such a degree that
just eating constituted a party.

One form of relaxation we had was to talk about astrology. When people knew I was an astrologer, they would
come to ask what the stars foretold. Nearly everyone getting
his orders for active duty came to me, and we tried to laugh
about charts, fortune-telling, and psychic phenomena. Many
men had an intuitive feeling that they would never come
back, and it was a sad time to be doing horoscopes—a far cry
from the glorious days of the Riviera. No one had much money and fees were never mentioned; it was an extra service
provided, half in jest and half seriously. But all the soldiers
and sailors were generous, and I collected plenty of cigarettes

and bottles of rum, which I could never learn to drink in those days, but could share or trade with someone else.

There were more top military brass on the island than I had ever seen before, and most of them came to have their charts made, including Commander Roger Keyes, who was to become a hero of naval history. No one bothered much with protocol or introductions. Under the influence of war, the Hebrides had a strangely silencing effect on everyone there. We were cut off from the world. There were no newspapers, and the few letters that came erratically by boat became a major event in our lives. We could not tell our relations where we were, for we were on active secret service. Occasionally I saw Ian Fleming again, more dour now than when I had first met him, always busy, always arriving unexpectedly and disappearing as quickly as he had arrived.

Sometimes it seemed as if everyone in the world had forgotten us, except the faithful Luftwaffe. They strafed us and we fired back, yelling like fishwives at the sight of swastikas too close for comfort. How our two-by-six island was not completely sunk into the sea I shall never understand, because the German planes scored numerous hits on the warships hidden away in the fjords of the other islands. Every day the grapevine brought us news of disaster; we never seemed to get any good news. All the men we knew seemed to get killed or never came back again, and we could not visualize the day when we might live in a world without war. For us, it was indeed the end of the world as we had known it. None of us could ever get back our youth or return to a society that knew debutantes and hunt balls, where girls were expected to look pretty, be entertaining, and provide good company for young men, who would court and hopefully marry us. We gave our youth, our ambitions, and in some cases, our lives; many of the nurses I knew got killed. Those in the home city of London were the worst hit, but somehow Elizabeth Bowes-Lyon and I survived and took a train back to Netley. Our smart navy uniforms were almost threadbare and had deteriorated during exposure to salt air. We cut each other's hair, forgot what makeup looked like, and wore sensible flatheeled brogue shoes made presentable by the application of spit and polish, which all good soldiers know how to do.

Then it was all over, except the shouting in the towns, celebrating peace, and the signing of national agreements. The only thing to do was to pretend the nightmare had never happened, and even to this day, I can bring down a shutter on my mind about the events of the "war to end war." Elizabeth Bowes-Lyon married a Chevalier of an ancient French house and became the mistress of a castle in Ireland and an enormous chateau in France. I hope her husband bought her another tiara, for the girl deserved it. She was a classic example of how tough a member of an old family can be when faced with unexpected adversity.

Many members of the sixtieth section of the London Red Cross got medals. I had several, and I hated the sight of them. In a war, the best reward is to be able to breathe free air again and know that one is alive. I ceremonially buried mine in the New Forest at the first sabbat I was able to attend after the war. Perhaps it was theatrical to do this, but it was like burying myself, and then, through the help and the renewal of psychic forces, being reborn in my beloved New Forest.

Our house had survived, but many young members of the family had either been lost in battle or were known to be killed. Nothing could ever be the same again for any of us, but we had to rebuild on what we had left. All the beautiful flower gardens, once the pride of the house, had been plowed under to make room for growing more food, and we never got the place to look like its old luxurious self. Besides, we had little money by now, and the fields of vegetables were needed to provide income. We had a home, a roof over our heads, and hope, not merely in the future, but in ourselves as individuals and as a family; we faced the need to survive. Most of the horses and dogs had died, and breeding activities had been cut down because of the lack of food, but we started off again with more livestock. Every year we built up a better herd of cattle; we had more goats for milk for the home, and hunting and polo ponies, and game dogs to keep dear old Roger's strain going. It takes many years to feel at peace after a war; the insecurity of doodle-bug bombs, air raids, and the aura of death are not easily expelled from the system.

We started to go back to the south of France, but it was not the same. Gradually plaques began to go up all through the streets of Nice, indicating that this was the place where perhaps a sixteen-year-old boy had been hung by the Gestapo, or where the Maquis—the French resistance group—had been exterminated. Foreign royalty drifted back, and again I drew horoscopes for them, but now there was little joy in it. Money was scarce, presents were impossible, and the days of easy money to be spent lavishly on just about anything I fancied were as dead as my youth. War is a blot on the conscience of any nation, as well as the individuals caught up in its web of intrigues. For me, it almost blotted out many horizons of thought and a lot of my life in astrology.

CHAPTER

The Swing of the Astrological Pendulum

After the war, a new breed of people became interested in astrology, and I was caught up in a fresh whirlwind of excitement. Titled names became unimportant—that is, if one is looking for names of historic renown, such as one once found in the great houses of Europe. Equally so, many of my army clients only had numbers, and these too were unimportant. Instead of being an astrologer for high society, I was down to earth with a new group of people.

Everyone I knew had problems—most of these problems were due to the war in one way or another—and astrology seemed to be the best way to get these problems solved. Rehabilitation was a major part of the new peace program. People were left just as bewildered by the attempt to resume a peaceful way of life as they had been when they prepared for war. During the war, everyone was alerted for action; now it was time to think about living peacefully again, but there were problems, such as how to rehabilitate the men returning from the forces, and how to get families together again. Women had changed and were capable of taking control of just about everything. Many women were reluctant to give up their professional status and return to keeping house for men who had become strangers.

Everywhere I turned, people were in a state of emotional turmoil. The movement of refugees from the city to the country during the war was supposed to be a temporary move designed to keep young children and the elderly in a place of safety. Some wanted to return to urban living, but quite a few had adapted well to country life, especially teenagers, who now wanted to stay in the country and do farm work, even when their parents wanted them to return to the cities.

The effect of the war was noticeable even in the way people ate. Even though food became more plentiful, the old habit of being frugal was still maintained. It seemed almost a sin to eat three good meals a day, much less leave any scraps on the plate. Another change was that my new group of clients did not want to know about their love lives. Some had become emotionally impoverished, others had known a new type of sexual freedom in the war, and still others were scared of loving anyone, but love was something they felt they could cope with. Where to go and what to do were the real problems. Skeptics who had not thought of consulting anyone about their future, because during the war there seemed to be no future beyond tomorrow, were hesitant now to take on the responsibility of making their own decisions about the type of life they wanted to lead. Fortune-tellers, psychics, and astrologers found a ready business from all these people and became a crutch for an insecure society that was hesitant to come to grips with peace.

I did numerous family horoscopes. I compared them and worked on the art of synthesis, trying to bring my clients back to a more harmonious way of life by pointing out the potential in their natal horoscopes. Peace was hardest for the men born under the fire signs of Aries, Leo, and Sagittarius, because they loved all the action going on in wartime, and for all too many, peacetime represented long periods of inactivity and unemployment. I found that many of these men were best helped by pointing out that they should go into business for themselves. One man in Dorset decided to learn to be a blacksmith, not with a view to shoeing horses, but to making artistic wrought-iron work. He has a big foundry now, and his wrought-iron works of art find their way to many overseas families. Another client invented and perfected a special type of irrigation now greatly used in Africa, where drought was, and is, a major hazard to farming.

The air signs were the hardest to deal with, but many managed to stay in the local aircraft plants. One was a brilliant designer who had an amazing chart full of adventure. He had the same birth date as Ian Fleming. I could almost see a whole new era of daring deeds unfolding before my eyes as I looked at his chart, but at the time he came to me, he felt his life's work was over. He ended up going to the Arab states as a flying instructor, fulfilling his potential for both traveling and an adventurous life. Occasionally he would return to England, look me up, and give me an account of his robust adventures. He became my "agent" in the Arab states and sent me many horoscopes to do.

One was for the man who became King Hussein of Jordan, whose astrological life I looked after for many years. His emotional life was as tense as his political and regal life. Many years later, I met the film actress living in Hollywood who caused such an impact on his romantic life and nearly brought a scandal to his royal house, which his aides were quick to hush up. I met her at a time when her own life was in a mess with love affairs gone wrong, and she had a small son to look after. She always had an ache in her heart for her old love, the King. He with the Sun in Scorpio, and she with the Sun in Taurus, had all the ingredients for a long-lasting love affair, but there were enough afflicted planets in both charts to make such a love a sordid, miserable mess in which neither would know happiness. Marrying two other mates did not solve their problem. As the years rolled on, King Hussein had much more than his love life to manipulate. He has a certain doomed quality about his life. Already he has survived several attempts to assassinate him, but his throne is frequently in jeopardy, and his political power shows signs of waning.

When considering love, the fifth house in a horoscope is important. It is the natural house of Leo and the Sun, and since ancient astrologers believed that the Sun god was also the god of life and love, they assigned the fifth house to love and children. The fifth house is important in sex and love relationships because it is the house where an expansion of consciousness comes about through emotion. The awakening of the fifth house in male and female charts brings the subjects newer and wider experiences, for they are put into contact with the source of life, whereas they were creatures of reason and limited feeling before. In the fifth house, reason— so important to the third house of Gemini—may be swept aside by sex and love. This love does not always conform to the social and moral concepts that society demands, for the love may be for a person of either sex or may be a mystical ecstasy through religion. The latter is becoming increasingly evident in horoscopes done over the last ten years, especially in subjects who also show artistic tendencies and have Venus placed in its natural home of Taurus. Because of many strange connotations, the fifth house needs very careful study by astrologers today, for it may not always mean a tremendous romance at a certain period. It could well mean that a subject is likely to be swept up into a cosmic consciousness through the new trends in religious fervor we are experiencing today. When the love is directed toward another person, not only the fifth house conditions must be taken into account, but the aspect of Venus must be found. It is in the workings of Venus that the refinements of love are discovered. If there is no aspect to Venus, but one to Mars, then you can be sure that there is a very passionate nature in which sex dominates the softer feelings of love.

Everyone seems to be interested in love, but the wise astrologer must always be aware that there are many deviations in this vast subject, and consequently many pitfalls. Long ago, I learned never to sit in judgment on any of my clients. One man's love may be another person's idea of obscenity, and a complete perusal of the horoscope is necessary to find out and understand the formula for the ingredients of love. Everything can be found within the fifth house: romance, courtship, and magnetic attraction ranging from mere sensation to the loftiest emotions. The enthusiasm and rapture of the subject may be directed not only to another person, but to music, art, or religion. To consider the fifth house only in terms of normal love is dangerous because we are living in times when the norm is likely to change from decade to decade.

A lesser known attribute of the fifth house is perhaps especially important today: the fifth house also indicates children, the product that a man leaves to posterity. The Sun, Mercury, or Mars in the fifth house can indicate the impossibility of having children by normal means, or it may mean that very few are likely to be born. Mars, in particular, indicates that there can be great difficulty in raising children. Saturn also limits the number of children, which often brings sorrow to the subject of the horoscope. The fruitful planets are Venus, the Moon, and Jupiter, but in the question of children, the eleventh house must also be studied. The sign on the eleventh house cusp, its ruling planet, and the planets in this house, are very important.

Strange emotional arrangements are cropping up in more and more horoscopes today. The case of a young man falling in love with a woman older than himself, however, is fairly constant, and I have known this aspect since my days as an astrologer on the French Riviera. It certainly does not reflect the gigolo theme, as so many novels would have us believe. Many such relationships have been mutaully beneficial to both parties, although they may not become as romantic and historic as the famous affair between the composer Frederic Chopin and the writer George Sand. Chopin had an Ascendant at 10 degrees in Virgo, and George Sand's Saturn hit this Ascendant, showing that her appeal to him was that of an older woman with good business sense. Chopin's Saturn was in trine to George Sand's Venus in Leo, so he was emotionally attracted to her over a long period of time, but he found it hard to demonstrate this attraction. Despite the many romanticized versions of the love affair of Chopin and Sand, astrologically it is likely that this was indeed a love affair, but hardly a sexual one. The two had a profound, secret understanding that no judgment along normal lines could possibly understand.

Comparing the charts of two people in love is still very important, and an astrologer looks for the following favorable things:

1. The sun of one chart on the Moon of the other;
2. A good aspect between the Sun in one chart and the
   Moon in the other, remembering that a trine or tri-
   angle, is regarded as a good aspect whereas a square
   is not;
3. Any aspect between the rule of the Ascendant in one
   chart, and the ruler of the fifth house or the ruler of
   the seventh house in the other;
4. Aspects of planets in one chart to Venus or Mercury in
   the other.

Bad aspects from Saturn to Venus or the ruler of the seventh house causes delays in marriage and may prevent it entirely.

Bad aspects from Mars to Venus or the ruler of the seventh
house cause fights before the marriage and should be regarded as a warning of things to come, and divorce is likely. When
Mars has good aspects to Venus, marriages at an early age are
likely.

Many of my clients used to worry because they did not
have any children; now many are worrying because they do.
Neptune, my least favorite planet, is generally the cause of
both kinds of trouble. Neptune in the fifth house often
brings peculiar conditions regarding children. It rarely provides any stable benefits under affliction. It is concerned with
disappearances and separations, elements that are increasingly
cropping up as family life strays more and more from the
norm that was established before Pluto was discovered in
1930.

I also did the horoscope of a man called Colonel Gamal
Abdel Nasser, who helped to eliminate still another client of
mine from the royal throne of Egypt. Nasser was born at
4:28 A.M. on January 15, 1918, in Alexandria, Egypt. He

was born to live with power and die because of it. He had a Sagittarian Ascendant and Libra at his Midheaven, and his whole horoscope reeked of involvement with the military, with arms, and with a way of life connected with aggression. That he died not from an act of aggression but from a heart attack in his own home is something that will always remain a surprise to me, but he did survive several attempts at assassination, as his horoscope showed.

I predicted his death within eight hours of the event, at a cocktail party given by the editor of *Tempo* magazine in Houston to celebrate my son's marriage. Among the guests, mostly from the newspaper world, was a man who had once been a consul at the Egyptian Embassy in New York. Our talk turned to the Arab-Israeli war and the fate of Egypt, and of course to the man who ruled Egypt so powerfully, Nasser, my old client. I had not looked at his horoscope for some time, but some psychic urge made me tell the company that Nasser would die of a heart attack before the end of the month. I gave the date but was about eight hours off—perhaps because I was working on Houston time.

Everyone was excited by my prediction, and several of the newspaper people made a note of the date, probably hoping to call me up on the date and say I was wrong. Several queried the means of his death; they thought he was more likely to die of cancer because they knew he had been in Russia to have a special cobalt treatment for this grim disease. When I got home that night, I pulled out the old horoscope of President Nasser, which I had prepared when he was a colonel, long before he took over the government of his country. What I had felt psychically was confirmed in the horoscope: Nasser was near death. Before the end of the month, there was a new President of Egypt. I predicted that the new President would be subject to an assassination attempt within a year. This happened in April 1971. He quelled the opposition and punished the conspirators, but there are signs that another attack will be made within a few months (but he will live for several more years).

There are indications in the national horoscope that the United States, rather than becoming less involved in war, will take a more active part in the affairs of the Middle East as well as in southeast Asia. Astrology students should find this worth looking into again at the end of March 1972. By 1977, the United States is likely to be facing one of the major crises in its history. The main problem internally will be racial, but externally there will be a threat from Moslem countries and communism. The ideological clash may well turn into a violent armed conflict, but the United States will always remain a bastion against communism. I doubt if the current President of Egypt will be in evidence at this time, but while people in high places may be expendable, ideologies are not. There will soon have to come a dramatic eyeball-to-eyeball encounter when the United States will need a touch of the "third eye" in order to keep pace with espionage activities and the infiltration of communism both within and without its borders.

After a period of trying to help the rehabilitation of my new class of clients, I found myself doing a number of communal horoscopes that related to business ventures. I received a telegram from the south of France asking me to work out a problem involving the merger of a famous vineyard in France with a British company. Sorting this out, I informed then that it would be a great business transaction with huge financial yields. I was supposed to have had a few shares given to me in the company, but it never came to pass—indeed, a sign of the times. In the old days, no one mentioned money, but it was a mark of honor to do something for the astrologer.

That honorable instinct seemed to pass away after the war. The new clients made many promises, were profuse in their thanks, but had short memories. I did not make a dime out of the vineyard horoscope, and today I get a trauma when I check the ever-rising price of the shares. Anyway, it was a lesson to be learned and profited by. It may seem mercenary to ask to be paid in advance for doing a horoscope, but it is the only way to work. I have no qualms about making this point when I give people details of what is required in order to set up a horoscope. In addition to having the date of birth, the place, and if possible, the exact time, I also like to have a check.

Recently I did the horoscopes of an entire family in Canada. They did not send their check at the time of booking the horoscopes, and I foolishly forgot to stand by my own rule. At first glance, the horoscopes looked so interesting that I got too involved, and only when I had finished and sent them off did I regret my action. Like gambling debts, astrology charts have to be paid for, and today my two children—both Virgos, with a keen appreciation of money and an even keener one of honor—are quite prepared to send out bills for anything I miss out on (but not without castigating me gently for my ineptness). Money has never truly been a problem to me because I can generally write or do horoscopes to keep a whole herd of wolves from the door, but I like to be financially secure, and periodically become very firm with clients about paying. After all, many of my clients today are professional men, and if I needed a doctor, a lawyer, or a dentist, I doubt if I could get one without paying. Professional laborers are worthy of payment for their services, and astrologers should come within this rule. Men often come to me and ask me to look into business trends for the next few years. They say they are interested in little else, but astrologers have to make up a complete chart in order to see where different patterns merge and affect other parts of life.

Planets in both Aries and Taurus affect business trends, but often the horoscope of the city or the national horoscope has to be explored, as well also the nature of the business. It is amazing how many people come to me with business worries, and all too often it is because they are in business pursuits that are running out of favor. In some cases it is possible to advise them to make a small switch.

One man I knew had a small tool business that did not thrive, but when he went ahead with a modification of the ancient crossbow (of all things), he obtained a new lease on his financial life. Finances are linked with business, of course, and it is really the financial status that people want to have analyzed. Jupiter, the planet of expansion, is very involved with the uplifting of fortunes, while a badly placed Saturn can restrict or hinder the same fortune.

The personal horoscope, the horoscope for the time when the specific company was formed, and the national horoscope are of the utmost importance in the final consideration in every case. The crisis caused in August 1971 by President Nixon's statement about the dollar was linked with the eclipse of the Sun in 26 degrees of Leo on August 20, 1971, aided by the lunar eclipse of August 6. When I left for a vacation in England at the time, I left a list of the eclipses on the blackboard in my kitchen for my children, with a column giving the potential effects—health and national finances would be affected. I also wrote down that the people most affected would be those with planets in 26 to 28 degrees of Leo, Aquarius, Scorpio, and Taurus.

We had also been doing various hososcopes connected with Japan for inclusion in my *Astrology Journal*. As we now know, President Nixon's attempt to save the dollar greatly affected the Japanese economy, and I think many of the inventive Aquarian Japanese have suffered great financial losses.

I frequently have to consider all national trends whenever doing a financial horoscope on a personal level, and my new client was no exception. My client was wealthy, if his good suit, elegant Mark IV car, and expensive ring and watch were taken as evidence of his financial status, although I am well aware that some of the best confidence tricksters in the world are also the best-dressed men.

His horoscope showed that he would never be without money, but it also showed that he could expect a steady decline in business during the next two and a half years. When he read this in the written report, he was furious, and he called me back to say so. I explained everything in simple language and then asked him what business he was in. I was informed that he was in the sort of business that could only increase as long as sex was in the world. This intrigued me, and even though he seemed reluctant to disclose the name of his business, I carefully made a point of quizzing him. Finally he told me that he manufactured contraceptives. For a moment, I began to wonder if I ought to recheck the chart, but some instinct made me press my questioning further. It turned out that he made only condoms, and I realized that we were talking at a time when "the pill" was just about to make a mammoth impression on the world. Within two and a half years, the pill was flourishing, and the sale of condoms was drastically reduced.

In the United States, against all advice and applications of logic, I established my Businessmen's Astrological Bureau. Everyone in business has a financial adviser; even so, the financial advisers came for astrological advice, and so did the principals of business. Several companies put me on a yearly retainer (a small one, to be sure, but it represented a sound income). My clients were limited in number, but had a diversity of business activites; one man made small parts for cars in Detroit, another was a furrier, a third was a vitamin-food specialist, and there was a health- and organic-food company with acres of land it hardly knew what to do with. We managed to foresee the boom coming in the use of organic foods, and after years of hard work, they are well on the way to being financially in the black.

My best client was a man in Los Angeles who was ultra-ambitious and was gradually building a small empire in the business world. After I did his horoscope, he was the subject of many articles in magazines and had a phenomenal rise to success. Checking his chart a couple of years ago, I was upset to find that he was not only going into a financial decline, but he might die, even though he was quite young. He barely managed to weather the storm when Wall Street hit a new low in April 1969. He confided to me that he felt he could rally—there was a temporary one in his chart—but then his life ran out. He died a few months after, and left behind a number of failing industries. I doubt if anyone is left in the company with the enthusiasm and talent necessary to restore it to its former heights of profitable fame.

Everyone was mad on astrology by fall of 1968, and it was fashionable to have a chart done. Hollywood, strangely enough, never yielded its filmstars to me. I think they went to Carroll Righter, but as my Businessmen's Bureau increased, I had more clients than I could cope with. I saw small private industries flourish, reach their apex, stagger, and die away. Businesses mushroomed and had their small moment of fame, then died away (as did some of the clients), but many flourished and parlayed their small private transactions into million-dollar concerns.

People in business generally appreciate their horoscope most when business is at its lowest ebb and they are wondering which way to turn, or if they have to stay at the bottom of the totem pole. There was little of the old faithfulness between client and astrologer, such as I had known in the early days in the south of France. Sometimes I would dutifully call a client to ask him to be careful on certain dates. My telephone was always on the go in the fall of 1968, for it was evident that the national financial situation would be at its most critical stage near April 1969, following another eclipse pattern.

It certainly did, and I am grateful that only one of my clients really lost a substantial amount of money. Most of them dutifully pulled out of the market when I indicated it was the right time. One was actually a personal friend, a woman with the Sun in Cancer—always a bad sign for me to associate with. She had been on cloud nine, going from one financial success to another, and could not believe that she could ever be caught in the turmoil of falling prices on the stock exchange. Typical of her tenacious sign, she hated to give up anything that she possessed until the last moment. By the fall of 1969 she was selling her large house, unable to pay taxes and having great difficulty in making ends meet. She came back to me, a tearful mass of wayward Moon-childishness, feeling that everyone in the world had done her wrong. She was born only to be a comet in the world of business. The last I heard from her, she was heading for Mexico to start a gift shop, with all the assurance in the world and a new boy friend as her backer. Reports from friends who visited the area later said that no gift shop was in existence at the address she had given me when she left with cries of "Now be sure to visit me." I heard that her husband divorced her and that her son headed to Haight-Ashbury to find his salvation and freedom.

Men have always been my best clients. Sometimes, when a woman asks me to do her business horoscope, I am reluctant to do so, because it is generally women with the Sun or Moon in Cancer who seem to migrate to me. I do not seem to have the patience to listen to all their trends in life, and for many of them, the horoscope is only a catalyst to hours and hours of endless gossip. No matter what they pay, it is never enough to make up for lost time, which should have gone into writing. I am not fond of providing a shoulder to cry upon and a back to bear their many burdens, as well as a horoscope.

I suppose it is wrong for an astrologer to have an antipathy to any sign. Only Cancer females can work destructive elements into my life, though. After all, we astrologers also have people who are compatible and incompatible to our own horoscopes, and, therefore, to our way of life. Few women born with the Sun or Moon in Cancer can ever divorce themselves from personalities, and emotions run high. Everything has to be ground down to an intimate level, whereas the men were brisk and businesslike and wasted little time on trivialities. They would read their horoscopes, ask reasonable questions, and not allow their romantic adventures to intrude on business. In my lifetime, I seem to have gone through a full circle of clients. I began with the intimate cozy days of the royal horoscopes in France, moved on to politicians, and after the war, to rehabilitation, on again to the very cold and impersonal form of astrology of my Businessmen's Bureau.

CHAPTER 7
The Authors' Curse

When I was living in Europe, it was a very simple way of life.
I got a commission from a publisher, delivered the book, and
then sat back and waited to see what happened. At its best, it
might be well-reviewed in the literary section of the London
Times, and followed by interviews and reviews in magazines.
At its worst, the critics would pan it in a review or ignore it.
So, apart from a few moments of tension waiting for the
reviews to come out, being an author in Europe was a very
genteel, tame affair compared with doing exactly the same
work in the United States. In Europe one writes a book,
waits for the reviews, and picks up the royalties. This was the
formula for successful writing, and I lived with this formula
for years. Some radio and TV studios used to have a regular
book-review feature, but it was rarely necessary for the author to be present, and they made a welcome release from
routine.

The whole tempo of a writer's life changes in the United States. Once a book is written and the publication date is set, then the panic buttons have to be pushed. The author has to get involved with the book on strange terms—she has to go out and sell it to the public. The publisher arranges a promotion tour for this purpose. Owners of bookstores like an author to go on tour, and it is quite a selling point for the book salesman if he can say that a certain author will appear in a number of towns on the network shows and will be available for interviews. It is a clever form of advertising, but it is not entirely free of financial obligations, since the publisher certainly spends a lot of money when he sends an author on tour.

It is really a mark of honor when the publisher decides to promote a certain book. Look through any catalog and you will find many, many titles, but you will probably recognize only a handful of authors. I have been fortunate with my publishers; they have chosen to promote my books, and so, between us, we have pushed up those vital financial figures so that the computers come out to prove that a Leek book is selling.

I have to justify the publisher's faith in me, and this means saying good-bye to the typewriter (with more and more reluctance) and taking to the air on a six weeks' promotion tour that can only be rivaled by the tours made by politicians in Presidential election years. A naïve author, unexposed to the mechanism of the publicity department of the publishing company responsible for the tour, might be very impressed at the number of towns visited. But make no mistake—the publisher is not interested in giving an author a sightseeing tour. Every stopover, every appearance, had better yield results in terms of increased sales in the area, or both the publisher and the author are in trouble. Of course, some authors lend themselves to being exposed to so much publicity. I know I am regarded in this light, probably because of the professional experience I had in radio and television in Europe and because of my extroverted personality. My first tour was for *Diary of a Witch*, and I was appalled by the idea of going out and talking about my own book.

Also, a strange thing happens to me when I have finished a book—I seem to become detached from it, probably because I write at a frantic pace. When a book is finished, I want to get it to the publisher as soon as possible, and I even hate to do the necessary revision. It is like a letdown from a drug when a book is finished; I become high with writing, and the only thing to do in order to avoid depression when I finish is to start another book. I used to have an alternative precaution against this peculiar form of depression: I would manage to get away to a totally different place. Now I have an energetic agent who produces contracts as quickly as I can write books, so I get away less frequently. In one way, writing is the state most authors prefer, but writing actually causes a strange, new life style that I am only now able to cope with and still feel like a human being. I am always surprised when someone tries to pin me down about how long it takes to write a book. I never think of books in terms of time. I say what I have to say in terms of chapters, and when there is no more that can be said on the specific subject, the book is finished.

Going on tour takes me away from the typewriter, which, as I grow older, is my major form of happiness. I used to know artists who knew their ultimate satisfaction in painting a picture, and now I feel the same about writing. It is a creative effort that is completely satisfying at the time, almost like a love affair. Going on tour for *Diary of a Witch* was an experience, and I had an opportunity to see how interviewing

on radio and television differs once the fish pond of the Atlantic has been crossed.

Few interviewers do any homework, so they usually meet
the author quite cold. Seeing the word "witch" in the title of
my book gave many interviewers the impression that *Diary of
a Witch* was a book about witchcraft. Actually it was an autobiography in which I tried to blend all the aspects of my life.
Anyway, despite some strange interviewing that made me feel
uncomfortable and sorry for the interviewer, my *Diary* managed to make it with the public in the popularity stakes. It
still sells, many years after its original publication. On that
first tour, I liked "Long John" Nebel, Bob Kennedy of WBZ,
and Mike Douglas best of all. They had a direct approach to
the interviews, and I felt the public really learned about the
book and about us. This does not mean to say that these
interviews were of the easy, friendly, cozy "join the club"
sort. These three interviewers seem to realize that the inter-
viewee has a point of view, and this is why she has been invited on the show. So, although they are all tremendous personalities in their own right, they are clever enough to restrain themselves. The result is informative entertainment.

It helps me to know the birth sign of the person interviewing me. John Nebel, born with his Sun in Gemini, probes for
answers and allows a line of thought to be developed. I never
mind clowning with Mike Douglas, as he is a ready wit himself, and I am quite capable of parrying some of his nicely
barbed questions. But the late Joe Pyne was my *bête noire*,
and I see no reason to gloss over his aggressive, rude personality just because he is dead now. I doubt if he ever read a
book before an interview, and his program was typical of a
strain of interviewers who once flourished on the West Coast.
Les Crane tried to be aggressive, but it did not come easily to
him. He's a nice person who was misled by a bad production

decision to mold him into an aggressive image just because it was the "in" thing at the time. Good interviewers are not molded; they develop a format and a style of their own, and the wise producer allows this to come about naturally. Alan Burke was also an aggressive interviewer, but on a more intellectual level. He seemed to have a tremendous sense of discrimination between the real and the phoney, and he was interested in social justice. Everyone thought he would tear me to pieces on the various interviews we have had together, but I always found Alan a wonderful person both off and on camera. One thing about people like Bob Kennedy and Alan Burke, born with the Sun in Virgo—they respond to sweet reason and respect anyone who presents an honest case, even if the subject, such as witchcraft, is controversial.

Women interviewers are a special breed in the United States. There are very few strong ones, who interview in depth. They rely on, and are conscious of, their own charm, and they display their charm to the full on camera and rarely press home a good point that perhaps the audience would like to see developed. Virginia Graham has always been delightful to me, probably because she senses that I respect her. She is conservative and charming, but when she feels she is right, she sticks with it and never loses a point. She can also continue to smile when delivering a punch line designed to reduce some guests to a nervous wreck. I always think Virginia has a complete confidence in her own life, and not just at the time when she is performing. Anyone who has read her autobiography must respect this woman who had a personal fight against a dreadful disease and survived without an atom of rancor in her. She is a comfortable, matronly figure with just enough glamor and wit not to antagonize the American housewives who comprise her major viewing audience. They relate to Virginia; when she is against abortion and free love, they probably nod their heads in approval; when she says coloring hair gives a woman a lift, they know she is right. She is a blessing to any author who goes on her program because she knows why the author is there, and she never forgets to give the book a good plug.

I loved appearing with Betty Hughes, the wife of Governor Hughes of New Jersey. We had a riotous time doing some cooking on her show. Unfortunately, I have never been used to the wild mechanical gadgets that are a feature of American kitchens. While my soufflé was not a spectacular culinary success on the show, our antics—especially my handling a mixer for the first time in my life—were worthy of *I Love Lucy*. Never did so tiny a soufflé go so far: the mixer took off at high speed, and the ingredients flew out like snow-flakes into the range of the camera.

From the warmth and wit of Virginia Graham and Betty Hughes, it is a long way to Barbara Walters, the first lady of television interviewers. I found her cool and remote, and with some very bad notes about me from her scriptwriter. Many of the big network shows rely so heavily on what the research workers in the studios put before them that an unpredictable person like myself can literally throw a monkey wrench in the wheels and leave the interviewer spinning around, won-dering if the facts in hand are for the right person.

We got off on a disastrous course for my interview on the *Today* show. Miss Walters and I fought like cat and dog, but we made our peace during an interview on *Monitor*. We caught up with each other again at an authors' luncheon at Higbee's in Cleveland. Barbara and I were there with Bennett Cerf to give our little talks to the huge audiences that Hig-bee's attracts at their regular monthly literary luncheons. Barbara was promoting her own book and had just started on her promotion tour; I was at the end of mine, having whizzed through twenty cities in twenty-five days. In the office before the luncheon, she admitted that she was nervous, and she did not know how I could keep going on so many tours

Miss Walters is a classic example of a person who is much warmer off camera than on, but like Richard Dimberley of the British Broadcasting Corporation, she is a wonderful interviewer for great national affairs. Maybe she feels better with people at White House-level than with anyone else, for her interviews with Mrs. Eisenhower, and with President Nixon and his family have been models of beautifully prepared workmanship. She is also tremendously photogenic and is always worth watching.

NBC likes to have its interviewers in the studios about 6:30 A.M., a ghastly time for anyone to make an appearance. The last time I went on the *Today* show, I had to leave Philadelphia at one o'clock in the morning after doing a late-night show there. My publisher had arranged for a Cadillac with a chauffeur to drive me to New York, where I was to go to the Americana Hotel to freshen up. We arrived there at 3 A.M. to find that the desk clerk had given my room to someone else, although the booking had been made for at least a month. Part of the authors' curse is to find a room in New York, always busy and seemingly always full, at 3 A.M. I finally found one at 5:30, and just had time to take a shower and freshen up before I rushed to the NBC studios, knowing that if I was late, whoever was in charge of visitors would be having a trauma. I had done five shows the day before, rushing from Boston to Philadelphia and then on to New York just for the all-important *Today* show. It was hard to realize that so much had happened in exactly twenty-four hours.

No matter how well the publicity office of a big publishing company plans its tour for the author, something always goes wrong, and the author is thrown on her own resources. Generally a public relations person is allocated to look after an author, but I have always found that on hectic tours there is a point when the public relations man wears out and has to take to his bed, leaving the author to plod the lonely route to fame. I cannot say I am phased when this happens; in fact, I think I like to go around the cities on my own, because I like to pull myself together in between shows. This means periods of meditation and quietness with little talking. With a public relations man around, I always get a sense that they are lonely and want to talk. Such is my own nature that at the end of most tours I feel I have provided a big shoulder for the public relations man to cry on, and generally I end up hearing the story of his life and his troubles, and we share a mutual desire to sort them out.

I am the first to admit that an author's best friend on tour can be her publicity man, but again, I find a great change in the publishing world. Years ago, when I made my first big tours, the public relations personnel were totally professional, dedicated people, who had good training on Madison Avenue and knew all the contacts in their particular town. Today the escort provided is quite likely to be an office girl with little experience and of very little practical help. Having been concerned with public relations offices all my life, I really like to go ahead on my own. When situations deteriorate, as they generally do, I can usually handle things by myself, without having a fainting girl on my hands or a young man who always has to call the office for advice. I like a public relations man who has the Sun in Leo or Virgo, for I seem to get along best with these types. If he has the Sun in Leo, he can be relied upon to know his business; and if he has the Sun in Virgo, he generally pays attention to details, and it is in the small things that so much can go wrong on tours. Take, for instance, the airlines—and for my part, anyone can take the airlines, but not me! A PR man with the Sun in Virgo would always know that in the autumn the airlines make changes in their flight schedules. Not too long ago, I needed split-second timing, and I found that I had a batch of airline tickets worked out on the summer timetable instead of the winter one.

Few people in New York offices who arrange tours for authors seem to have much personal experience in traveling. Large companies rely on travel agents, and they, too, can make some horrible mistakes. They mislay a ticket for a connecting plane here and there while the office girls, eager to make out a full schedule to keep the author out of mischief, often forget that it takes time to get from one interview to another. Even though I know New York City better than London, I recently found out that it is quite impossible to keep a schedule in New York; so, if there are a number of interviews to be done in one day, they need to be carefully spaced out. Anyone who knows New York also knows that no city suffers more from complete chaos than this one when it rains. I did the whole New York segment of my 1970 fall tour in downpours of rain that kept up steadily from the first calls in the morning to the late-night shows. Chauffeured cars cost an arm and a leg, taxi drivers become nonexistent, and the glamorous world of the author on tour falls apart in one soggy mess. Interviews deteriorate from the moment she walks in, drenched to the skin, only to be told she had better hurry since the show is about to begin. I have yet to find a way to conquer New York and its rain and maintain a friendly attitude toward television studio personnel, who may not know, in their air-conditioned, windowless world, the perils of getting from one place to another on time; they sometimes begrudge an author five minutes to wring out her hair.

Wet weather in New York, bad traveling conditions, and

the constant repetition of horrid hotel service all combine to age an author on tour. Living as I do, in the shadow of the great space program of the United States, only twenty miles from the Cape Kennedy launching pad where a man can be sent to the Moon, I bitterly resent the deterioration in the airline services today. One can circle Atlanta airport for an hour and know the connecting plane is winging on its way; one can be held up at Kennedy for hours. We have to learn to accept this, but when it takes eight hours to get from Houston to Washington, and twenty-one hours from Florida to Edmonton, Alberta, then I think it is time we began a close review of prevailing conditions of flights in the United States. In all my years of traveling—I am on my second million miles of flying—I have noticed a tremendous deterioration in the airports and flights all over the United States and Canada. We still take a long time to get off the ground, and many hours can be spent each year waiting in line at airport counters to get a ticket validated or made out.

I travel first class not because I am class-conscious, but merely because there are some good waiting rooms for first-class passengers where the weary, travel-tired passenger can collapse with some degree of comfort when there is a time lapse or a plane missed. I know every nook and cranny of most airports, and there is a limit to the times one can visit the restaurant or study the literature on the newsstands. When I am on tour, catnaps in the first-class waiting rooms are generally the only means of rejuvenating myself and becoming fairly presentable for the next performance.

For the author on tour, the hotel room is the last refuge where she can pull herself together, collapse, and wonder what planetary patterns influenced her to make her a writer. But hotel service is becoming a thing of the past. I am amazed at the sameness of all the hotels throughout the

United States—a result, no doubt, of the franchise system that is taking over the hotel business. In New York City, the Waldorf-Astoria, the Plaza, and the Delmonico Hotel appeal to me, but publishers do not like to put their authors up in these last vestiges of elegant rest for the tired traveler. Apparently the large chains of hotels have a working agreement with publishers, who settle for some second-class places, even though they may have to pay first-class prices.

Most hotels have a check-out time of either 1 P.M. or 3 P.M., but I have frequently arrived at hotels about 6 P.M. to find the room not ready for me. Try to get into a hotel room in any town that has a major baseball or football game on! Despite booking well in advance, the poor author is still likely to find that hotel managers are not averse to hiring out rooms for a few hours to an influx of people in the town to see "the game"—which results in more income for the hotel or motel owners. Even a written guaranteed acceptance that there will be a room is no assurance. On one tour, I got very tired of being told to "do something for about two hours while the room is got ready." Desk clerks are adept at shrugging shoulders and dismissing the traveler, who has very little redress. I am inclined to agree with Barbara Walters, who wondered if it was all worthwhile when we were at the Higbee's luncheon.

Cleveland is one of my favorite cities to visit, despite the smog. I have been fortunate enough to be invited to do an autograph party at Higbee's store and have been very well looked after by the buyer for the book department, Miss Ann Udin, and her capable assistant, Richard. Nothing was too much trouble for them, and every trip went smoothly. The authors' luncheons are a great innovation: five or six authors are invited to address the large assembly of people who love to partake in the cultural activities of the city. After the luncheons, each author sells autographed copies of her books, and sales are always good. If every part of a tour were as well-arranged as the Cleveland segment, part of the curse on the author would be lifted.

For me, there is a special joy in visiting Cleveland other than selling books. I shall reveal a deep dark secret about my life—I am a railway buff! Rail transport has intrigued me since I was a child. Cleveland is a pleasant break from the routine of corralling cabs at airports to get to the hotels. I enjoy grabbing my small bag and typewriter and trekking just a little way from the airport to take a train that will take me right under the Higbee building. Keeping always under cover, I can then get to the Sheraton Hotel, and I feel a great thrill, unlike being disgorged at the front entrance by a cab. Also, this short rail trip gives me a chance to indulge in some nostalgia of the great days in the United States when ebullient millionaires had their own railcars and traveled in fine style. It was a status symbol that owning a private plane can never quite measure up to. Whatever the weather in Cleveland, I can forgive the city everything as long as it keeps up the railway from the airport to the netherworld of Higbee's.

I always check my horoscope before going on a major promotion tour. Several of my publishers understand this, and they put up very little opposition to arranging the date of the tour to suit my best astrological patterns for traveling. If there was ever a need to check a personal horoscope, it is definitely before making major journeys of several weeks. By any laws of logic, doing the amount of traveling that I do and living on the favorite route for hijackers, I should have been on at least one hijacked plane in the last two years. I was actually booked by a publisher to go on one flight that ended up in Cuba instead of Miami, but I had made my own arrangements in New York and changed planes.

Like the shoemaker's wife who often goes without shoes, a busy astrologer may forget to check her own horoscope, although she is careful to assess those of her clients. This happened to me early in 1971. I was due to discuss a business deal with Rod McKuen, which meant leaving Florida to catch him between tours (we had been skirmishing with each other for several months trying to find a date). I booked a flight from Florida to Los Angeles, to depart on February 8, 1971. David Melton, who was to be part of the deal with Rod McKuen, was to fly in from Philadelphia and we were to have a three-way conference.

On the night of February 6, I had the same dream I had had years before, when I was in Rabat, Africa, and managed to escape the earthquake there. I checked my horoscope and decided it was in bad shape for traveling on a major business venture, so I called David Melton in Philadelphia and suggested that he put off his journey as well. It was very early morning and perhaps he was just too tired to do anything but agree with me. Anyway, neither of us made the trip to Los Angeles; each of us spent February 8 thinking how near we were to a big financial deal. But I am a complete coward when it comes to earthquakes, and this was one of the reasons why I left Los Angeles, where I originally had a home. I had never gotten used to the chandelier shaking every month.

At 11:00 A.M. on the morning of February 9, I switched on my radio and heard the news that Los Angeles had been hit by a major earthquake at approximately 6:00 A.M. that morning. My regrets about the business deal faded away in a sense of relief. I tried to call McKuen, but it was impossible to get through to anyone in Los Angeles for several days.

Having done McKuen's horoscope, I was not unduly worried for his safety. But even without killing or injury, an earthquake can shake up the human system as effectively as it shakes up the earth. McKuen's horoscope showed he would have a small accident, and as a matter of fact, when we finally reached him, he was annoyed that he had injured his toe, but was otherwise fine and growling bitterly about how cowardly David and I were.

I can only practice what I preach, but the difficulty is that no one's life goes on a course entirely of its own making. The influence of environment and education also becomes tangled up with the zodiacal influences of other people, and sometimes it is difficult to follow the pure, direct lines of the horoscope, which shows the potential and the right way to go through life. In small everyday matters, others' free will can upset the potential of an individual horoscope, but on major matters, destiny plays a definite part. For instance, had it been my destiny to be killed in the Los Angeles earthquake, no amount of planning on my part would have avoided the issue. Some pressure would have been put on me so that I would step forth to fulfill my grim destiny. As it was, I had free will to cancel the plane ticket, and free will to risk upsetting a business deal of great financial importance. It's really like being given a new lease on life when things like this happen.

Our financial venture never really materialized, as Rod went on tour again. David had things to do in his art world, and I got involved in making cassettes, but at least my nerves had not been shattered by yet another earthquake. I suppose one day an organized promotion tour may well lead me again into a dangerous area, and I really must resolve always to check my horoscope. While many publishers accept their authors' whims and eccentricities, the new crop of youthful publicity personnel seems anxious only to get their work done and forget they have sent an author on tour. After being three weeks on tour, I called back to one office to find the chief of the PR department had left. No one even knew I was on tour, nor were they able to discuss a revision of the schedule. Once again I made my own arrangements.

On one fall tour, I did have the sense to check my horoscope before we even made up the tour schedule. There were five days right in the middle of the tour where I saw indications that I would be involved in litigation. I pointed this out to the public relations man, and my heart sank when I realized he was very new in his job and had little knowledge of me. He realized he was committed to arrange a tour of some six weeks' duration, and he was prepared to live by the letter of his own law.

I warned him I might have to break the tour in the fourth week, but he obstinately planned a full schedule. On the fourth week, while in Minneapolis, my lawyer in Florida called to say that some of our legal business was due for a hearing the next week. The Cincinnati, Chicago, and Pittsburgh part of my tour had to be cut. The PR man was mad, but I pointed out that I had warned him. The cancellation of the tour was not a major point of destiny, however; it was just the clash of two personalities.

Skeptics of astrology like to point out that people interested in the subject are forever reading their horoscope for every small thing in life and that the planetary patterns make them fearful slaves, scared to do anything without consulting the horoscope. The person who is well-versed in astrology and approaches it with a scientific attitude, knows that this is false. The horoscope is there to be used when necessary, just as umbrellas are there to be used if the weather forecast indicates rain. Few people are so fearful of bad weather that they always walk around clutching umbrellas or wearing over-shoes, and the same principle applies to astrology.

Major trends in life will always be there for the person to read. In most cases, his free will influences decisions; in many more cases, the contact and influence of other people in his life will also affect him. The horoscope will show the right way to go, the high and low cycles, and it is in catching these cycles at the right time that a horoscope becomes a useful map of life. It is available if one needs it, like the aspirins stored in the medicine cupboard for headaches or a hose for watering the garden during drought. No one is forced to take aspirins, water the garden, or look at the horoscope, but they are all there to be used as and when needed.

Some people think that religion and astrology are crutches on which they must always depend. This is not so. A crutch may be necessary, but both a religion and astrology work best when the subject begins to think for himself and be-comes capable of accepting the responsibilities that life brings along. Medically speaking, a crutch for a broken leg never completely solves the problem until the leg begins to be exer-cised and performs its function again. All too many people today turn to anything as a means of absolving themselves from making decisions or accepting responsibility. Flip Wilson, the amiable comedian, coined a good phrase when Geraldine, one of the characters he portrays, make an excuse for just about everything she does in life: "Oh, the Devil made me do it." This reflects the times and our attitude toward life, in which a sense of guilt about so many things pervades. Astrology and star-lore should not reduce us to a nation of excuse-making people afraid to make decisions or stand by them. If it does this, then it fails as it has never before failed in its six thousand years of history.

We can indeed accept responsibility for our own lives, but

other people and other circumstances affect us through the influence of the stars. It is when the influence of others is closest to us that we find our free will debilitated. For instance, most of us like to please people who are influencing our lives. It may be that the influence is greatest when people are in love, but it is certainly great with business associates, too. The wise author wants to please the publisher, but in dealing with the top echelon of publishing—the president, editors, and the public relations department—she may find herself in a quagmire, knowing what is really best for herself, but unable to fight the publishing world's equivalent of city hall.

During my numerous promotion tours for several of the top publishing companies, I have evolved a plan, aided by astrology, that helps me to survive the authors' curse and enables me to return to my family as a human being. The first principle, of course, is to assess the horoscope as soon as a date is given for the projected tour. If it is marked with very bad aspects, then it is up to me to fight the public relations office quietly but firmly, and point out that such and such a date would be better for everyone (always remembering, of course, that the money of an increased sale is what the publisher is after).

Having fixed a reasonably good date—and no astrologer can constantly expect to get perfect ones all the time—when the first batch of airline tickets arrive, I take time to check departure times myself, even if the tickets are issued by travel agents. They, too, may be having a few bad aspects in their charts. The arrival of the first schedule generally makes me wonder how any human being can travel so much and do so many shows and newspaper interviews. I am firm about having enough time to get my hair done, for personal appearances certainly matter, and few television producers like to have a travel-worn, bedraggled author rushing in to do her thing. (If an author is used to going to beauty shops, she should take time before the tour date to learn to do some basic fixing of her hair herself.)

Most tour arrangements work on the premise that everything is going to be perfect and that flight schedules run on time and that cabs are easy to obtain at airports. I dispel these illusions and point out that time on the ground is pretty important. Experience has shown me that to get into Manhattan from any of the New York airports is a major feat of ingenuity, and booking in at the hotel can clip anything up to an hour off the precious "free time" of a traveling author.

If an author has wanted to go on a diet but has never quite been able to do it, then a promotion tour becomes a natural way to do it. More and more hotels cut off restaurant and room service at earlier times at night. Frequently I have checked in at midnight when no food could be found anywhere in the hotel, and then I had to be out of the hotel before the coffee shop opened in the morning. So I take along an emergency kit of instant coffee and apples or cookies. It is definitely not safe to rely on eating on the planes these days, especially if an author is foolish enough to travel coach class. Airlines are cutting down on just about everything but the pilot these days, and food is the first thing to go. On a flight series of short hops, an author is lucky to see any food at all and may have to resist becoming an alcoholic, since liquor at times is the alternative to strange-tasting coffee and soft drinks that somehow manage to taste of laundry detergent.

The first temptation of an author going on the road for the first time is to remember that she has friends in many parts of the country. How nice it is to think of being able to contact them again. But there is no time for socializing left if the public relations man has done his duty. I beware of asking friends to meet me at the airport, for this is the quickest way to lose an old friend. With the erratic plane schedules, delays in the flight patterns become inevitable. Also, it is difficult to arrange meeting places at airports, since so many of them have undergone renovation to make room for the 747s. I'm firm about making dates only for the hotel, where I hope my room has been maintained for me after the usual 6 P.M. deadline. After the first few days on tour, the author's basic need is to keep herself in good health and a state of fitness in order to cope with more and more television and radio shows. I am fortunate, inasmuch as I can catnap just about anytime and need very little prolonged sleep. Recently I arrived in Edmonton, Alberta, after a twenty-hour journey, to do the late-night show of Tommy Banks. Morey Amsterdam was on the same show. The producer, Douglas McCrea, says it was quite a sight to see Morey and me fast asleep thirty minutes before the show; then we both woke up, shook ourselves, and went on as fresh as two daisies.

Catnapping is quite an art, and authors who need lots of sleep may collapse and forget to wake up, or be wakened, in time for a show. I always mistrust the local talent for directions. In the United States I have discovered that few people know their own cities well, and they work on the old-fashioned idea that the route from point A (the hotel) to point B (the studio) is as the crow flies. Cabs and public transport are erratic, so I allow plenty of time to get to the studios, as a late author can cause traumas for the producers of shows, and their nervousness can transmit itself to the author. Also, I allow for the vagaries of the weather. It may be sunny in Florida in February, but it is hellishly cold in Minneapolis and may be raining in San Francisco, and transport slows down accordingly.

Above all, I travel light as far as luggage is concerned, and I plan my wardrobe for the whole tour. It may be that I have a preponderance of late-night shows or too many day shows; dresses have to be planned accordingly. I am fortunate in that I always wear long dresses, and I can get a great variety of clothes packed by using muumuus and saris. I am also impervious to heat and cold, so I rarely have to make allowances for changes from the semitropics to other kinds of weather. An Irish mohair stole generally suffices as a top covering, although on one trip in Edmonton I was nearly defeated when I arrived after a ghastly, hazardous flight through heavy snowstorms, to find the temperature 3 degrees below freezing. It steadily deteriorated to 26 degrees below.

Breathing according to yoga principles and relaxing my body generally allows me to survive these extreme changes of temperature. I like to travel with one bag and my typewriter, with the bag of such proportions that I can haul it around myself, for despite our ability to send a man to the Moon, there is still an increasing element of chance for the air passenger who sends her baggage ahead and hopes that the bags will arrive at the same time at the same destination.

I have noticed that more and more people get on the plane clutching their belongings—and they are wise to do so. My worst experience in this regard was in the fall of 1970. I had gone through a couple of dozen flights always carrying my bag, but on this occasion I was taken to the airport in Melbourne, Florida, by a very well-known engineer from the Space Center. He had been plane-minded all his life and became quite angry when I did not want to release my single bag to the desk clerk. When I went to mail a letter at the airport, my enthusiastic plane buff announced triumphantly that he had sent my bag on the freight wagon to the plane and that I could travel in comfort for once. True, it is pleasant to go on board carrying only a pocketbook, but it is less

enchanting to arrive in St. Louis at 9 P.M. expecting to
change into a colorful dress to do a late-night show and then
find that the baggage has not arrived.

Losing baggage is a major disaster when an author is on
tour, and it can easily happen, since the tour consists primar-
ily of one day and night in any given place. I finally caught
up with my baggage a week later in Philadelphia, after I had
clothes sent to me and had purchased such things as makeup
en route. I never part with my typewriter under any circumstances, and now the same principle applies to my small traveling bag. Where I go, it goes, and this way we save both time
and temper at the numerous airports I flash through on a
promotion tour. Also, a small bag easy to carry is very important when an airport is hit by a cab or limousine strike, or
when the redcap service is nonexistent. It behooves the traveling author to develop a certain technique for traveling. Even
so, there are many times when she wonders if it is worthwhile, but the consolation comes when the royalties begin to
arrive. Didn't I say the name of the game was money?

CHAPTER

Publish and Be Damned—Then Distribute or Die!

On one of my visits to the United States about eight years ago, I could hardly wait to get off the plane in New York and set foot in Manhattan. My target was a group of businessmen, and I wanted to present to them an entirely new concept in merchandising. Clutching my large portfolio one morning, I explained exactly what the trends in marketing would be, and then sat back to wait for the approbation.

It did not come. Instead, there was gloomy silence, and I felt it was time to collect my portfolio and do a disappearing act.

"It's a great idea," said one of the men, "but it would revolutionize so many areas of thinking in the United States that we could not afford to be associated with it."

"Come to lunch," said another. "You're a bright girl, and I know we can find something else for you to do." The other four men said nothing, but looked as if they wanted me to go

and play on some busy freeway during the rush hour. I refused the luncheon engagement and had no desire to do anything other than what I had come to New York to do.

All I wanted to do was to use a large Madison Avenue advertising and publicity agency to market a complete series of
items of astrological merchandise, varying from giveaways to
several games with a planetary pattern. There seemed to be
no limit to what could be done; I had designs for birthday
cards, posters, expensive gifts, wearing apparel, tiny gifts for
dime stores, gold and silver things suitable for Tiffany's and
Nieman Marcus. What was wrong was that my vision of the
future was placed before men who could make money but
who had very little vision. They were in the same rut that
makes producers churn out the same old soap operas—no one
dares to change a successful formula. I could dream only on a
truly big canvas in those days. On my first visit to New York,
I had been struck by the quantity of astrology magazines
everywhere, and my second impression of them was that they
did not measure up to the thinking of the old German school
of astrologers that I followed. They seemed shallow productions, lacking scientific quality and geared to the cheapest
form of astrological entertainment.

I envisioned an astrology newspaper or magazine that went
into astrology in depth. I never wanted to wipe out the
others, for I believe they have a place, but I wanted just one
paper, at least, to put astrology in its right perspective as a
science.

My business friends turned down this idea, but a lawyer in
New York put me in touch with a dear old retired newspaperman called Ben. He was great. He helped get me back to a
positive way of thinking, and he said he would arrange an
interview with a friend of his who had once had an astrology
magazine years ago.

He took me to see Larry Herbert and we got on very well together at that first meeting. But a few phone calls discovered that while a couple of financiers liked the idea, they were not prepared to invest at the moment.

I returned to England, very disillusioned about the adventurous spirit of American businessmen, but I decided nevertheless to pack up and emigrate to the United States and start a small business concern of my own. The idea suited my publishers—I arrived with a flurry of publicity, two new writing contracts, and a good friend in Connecticut to visit until I got myself sorted out.

I got so busy writing that I almost forgot my big dream of merchandising. Sometimes I would look at my precious portfolio and wince that such good ideas were going to waste.

I had one or two setbacks in business, such as a meeting with the executive of a record company who persuaded me to make some tapes on astrology. Then he defaulted and took my tapes with him, despite pressure from lawyers. Also, as soon as I thought I was getting organized, my publishers wanted me to go on tour to promote different books. Ultimately the tours paid off, as I still get royalties on those early books, but royalties are paid twice a year, and sometimes it seemed a long time between payments.

Apart from the bad deal on the records, I showed a lot of my sons' designs to a textile company. The president talked to me, was impressed, and collected the designs. Sixteen phone calls and ten letters never resulted in my getting a reply from him or anyone else in his office. I was getting good training, if nothing else, in business tactics in the metropolis. All the lessons that I have profited from in my life I have learned in a dramatic way—it seemed that I had to be really kicked down into the gutter before I learned. The most consistent element of my life was writing. My excellent agent,

Roz Cole, gave me plenty of work and a lot of advice to forget merchandising—because I could really do as much writing as I wanted.

I pushed my merchandising dream to the back of my mind, but it was always a nagging dream, something that I had to attain before I could be completely satisfied. Fortunately, I had sense enough to write myself out of my misery, and I went on from success to success. Supplementing my writing were extensive lecture tours around the universities; usually I spoke about witchcraft, astrology, ESP, and religion in general. For a week, I was "Witch in Residence" at Washington University in Missouri. I had a great time there—rap sessions went well into the night with the students as well as the faculty. Everything I did at that time seemed to be successful except getting the merchandising program off the ground, and it haunted me more than any ghost did when I went with Hans Holzer, my parapsychologist friend, on numerous research expeditions in the United States and Europe.

I had been used to leading three lives in Europe: one involved in witchcraft and studying astrology; another, actively working and writing in television and radio; and the third as a successful businesswoman. I still needed the extra facets of myself in which I knew I could function well. WBZ studios, a Westinghouse-owned business in Boston, were always pleased to see me, and I did numerous programs for them with Bob Kennedy and Squire Rushnell.

When Bob was due to go on vacation for a month, Squire wanted me to take over the job while he was away. But the top executives in New York tabooed the idea, feeling that anyone known to be interested in witchcraft and astrology "might be bad for the sponsor's image." Now I see what an amusing thought that is, since the same sponsors come to me to do work for them in advertising.

One day about six years ago, my agent, Roz Cole, called me and asked if I could devise an entirely new concept for a new column on astrology for the *Ladies' Home Journal.* After two nights of thinking, I typed out a column, sent it in, and I got a monthly column with them. The pay was good and I thoroughly enjoyed every minute of it. I got away from the His and Hers thing and related astrology to all facets of living, and I updated it into twentieth-century terminology. I studied the planetary patterns each month and related them to fashion, interior decorating, sports, television, child care, health, cosmetics, and about fifty other subjects. The column was an immediate success and the first month (in the October issue) won an award from the New York Director's Guild for the best new approach to an old subject. Someone forgot to tell me about the award, but it was a pleasure when it finally caught up with me.

The column went on for about four years. Then there were editorial changes, and I was out in the cold. No one is more out than a one-time favorite columnist: the name goes out of the masthead, old contacts in the office are never available on the phone, and gradually the columnist learns an important fact of life as a writer—we are all expendable.

But I was not without a column for long, because I went to work for *Pageant* magazine. It is not as satisfying as working for the *Ladies' Home Journal* because I am back on the old His and Hers column. But a steady check each month seemed a good idea. I was tired of bashing my head against brick walls, trying to convince editors, who live very set, conservative lives, that astrology needs a new look and can still be popular if it does not follow the boy-meets-girl pattern. I had discovered that most newspapers and magazines, even those lurking behind a conservative masthead, want sex infused in all the articles. I now give the public what the editor thinks it wants—with the personal reservation that the public, in my opinion, is not the mass of morons the editors assume them to be. They should read my wonderful fan-mail which indicates people are interested in scientific astrology.

Contracts for more and more books consoled my loss of the *Ladies' Home Journal* column, and today I get a lot of mileage out of my old ideas. They are syndicated in many countries besides the United States: Finland, Japan, Australia, Portugal, Mexico, Belgium—every week a column of mine is sold to a foreign country. I have not yet seen the column in Japanese; it's a pleasure in store for me.

Many years ago, in Europe, I used to know a wire service reporter called Bill Dick. I ran into him in New York, where he told me he was working for the *National Enquirer*, and he added that this popular paper now had a new look. I began to do a column for the *Enquirer* in addition to everything else. Meanwhile, my plan of merchandising was going into action throughout the United States. Madison Avenue really went to town promoting astrology, and everywhere I looked I could see astrology motifs. Someone was certainly making money, but it was definitely not me. This was a blow, of course, but at least I had proved myself right.

Then I got a good break in the shape of a telegram sent to me in Houston. It was from Larry Herbert, asking me to come to New York to talk about starting the magazine on astrology that I had originally had in my portfolio. I took the first plane out.

Larry arranged for me to meet a man who was ultimately to join in our corporation. We formed Twin World Productions, Incorporated, with Larry Herbert, David Geller, and myself as equal partners. David agreed to finance the paper until it got off the ground, Larry did the layout, and I was in charge of the editorial side. We worked like mad to get a mock-up out, and through Larry's contacts, we got Kable News Company to handle all the distribution. Always concerned with the editorial side of production in my work, I had forgotten that the United States is a huge country, and some magic force has to be used to get astrology magazines from New York to thousands of other points so that all the newsstands are supplied. We had subscriptions too, of course, but selling on the newsstands was to be the life stream of our periodical. We got a good deal in having the magazine printed in Canada, and Larry made many trips to Montreal and returned with reports that the printing company was really bending over backward to be helpful. George Davies, then president of Kable News, was also doing a great job in getting major national distributors interested and in six months we had our first edition out.

There is quite a kick in seeing one's own brainchild appearing on the newsstands. One of the happiest days of my life was when *Sybil Leek's Astrology Journal* was born. We made mistakes, of course, and the worst one was the size of the magazine. We wanted to get away from the small-size astrology booklets, but we went overboard. The first issue came out with the soft cover of a newspaper and the size of the old *Harpers* magazine. Every newsstand owner in the country complained, so we reduced it to a semi-hard-cover format about the same size as *Time*, and in November 1971, to an even more convenient-to-handle size.

If you think the newsstand men were satisfied, you are mistaken. By this time, I realized I had either graduated into being a publisher-editor, or I had deteriorated into nothing. We had a good setup for success—a financier to back us, a hard-working staff in New York, myself doing publicity, and George Davies of Kable News really rooting for us. I visited major distributors all through the country and they were great too—the trouble was with the men who sell on the newsstands.

I knew why after my visits to many of them on the eastern seaboard. When we first went into production, there were about five pornographic magazines on the average newsstand; today there are about eighteen. Newsstands, if you notice, usually do not have much space, and we were slowly being squeezed out of circulation. The newsstand owners were often aggressive and rude and were always blunt: "Why should I sell an astrology magazine that might take three days to sell out when I can sell every bit of pornographic stuff I can lay my hands on?" said one dealer in New York. A dealer in Boston was definitely brutal: "I like my wife to have all she wants, and she wants plenty. The best way I can keep her happy is to give her plenty of spending money, and pornography means money to my family."

I almost laugh when I read the reams of paper about government studies on pornography. The fact is that the public is prepared to pay for what it wants, and the result is that many magazines are folding up. Make no mistake—pornography is here to stay and will be as long as people are willing to pay good money for a poor substitute for the real thing. At one time, people went to houses of ill-repute such as Chicago was once famous for; now it's cheaper to get all the thrills and divertissement for a dollar or so by purchasing a magazine. If the public wants pornography, the newsstand men will see that the public gets it.

We pulled together: Larry and George Davies doggedly worked hard on layout and distribution from the New York end, and I always plugged the *Astrology Journal* during my tours.

Well, with hard work and dogged determination, *Sybil*

Leek's Astrology Journal survived and will soon be in its third year of publication. We try to keep up our standard of writing, although we compromise a little by doing a day-by-day forecast called Predictoscope, and even without the co-operation of the newsstands, we are gaining ground every month on our circulation figures. We had one advantage: our advertisers are happy because we had a good pull with the public, and as all magazine people know, keeping the advertising going is one step in the right direction.

We still have to fight for every inch of space on all those newsstands, and I check them everywhere I go. Since I have been an editor-publisher, I have learned to meet fire with fire, and there are still some tricks to pull out of the old bag of magic so that the *Astrology Journal* does not concede any more space.

In the early days of the *Astrology Journal*, I went to the Atlantic Coast Independent Distributors' Association convention in San Juan, Puerto Rico, and addressed the distributors. They were completely cooperative, but I made the mistake of thinking we had won a big victory. The A.C.I.D.A. is a vital force in the life of all magazines, but all they can do is to send out parcels of magazines to their men, who in turn get them out to the newsstands. So we had cooperation at the top level, but not at the bottom. The trucking and rail strikes did nothing to help us either, and we survived by using private planes to get out one batch of magazines.

I had what I thought was another bright idea—to start an astrological dating service. We never intended this to be a marriage bureau; it was to be merely a means of getting some lonely people together. We advertised it as a service in the *Astrology Journal.* The idea was that we would compare charts and find people who had mutual interests and were linked by the common needs. We thought many people would get together and be pen pals, and we clearly stated this in our advertising data.

It was an experience I shall never forget, for in a brave moment I said I would personally attend to the comparison of charts. I did, and after a few months I was ready to look for some quiet place in which to have a nervous breakdown. No one can believe the situations that arose. One woman wrote to say it was time she had her three dates. When I looked up her application, I found I had not been able to find anyone compatible for her because she was 86 years old. If you have never tried to fix up an elderly and determined lady with a blind date, you have missed an experience.

More men than women applied to use the dating service, and soon I was beginning to see danger signs—especially when one man's horoscope showed that he was married and had several children. Others wrote their specifications, such as a man in Texas who was seventy and said he liked only young girls. He confessed he did not want to marry anyone because he was living on his own and had a wife whom he had not divorced. At least he was honest and saved us a lot of trouble. A few people wrote begging for a "true soul mate." One thing is for certain: there may be many lonely people in the world, but they are looking not for compatible friends, but for sexual satisfaction and extramarital affairs.

One week I had an application from a man in Canada with an unusual French name. A month later I had another letter with the same name. Comparing the two applications, I discovered that they were husband and wife. Each sent a covering letter asking me to send the names of the compatible people to addresses other than their own, since they did not want each other to know about their applications.

The astrological dating bureau was a strange experience and was not one I ever want to go through again. I worked

hard, comparing all those charts with the genuine intention
of helping people, but I guess I am not made to be a lonely-
hearts messenger. The day we stopped the dating service was
celebrated with a huge sigh of relief.

I had several good breaks in merchandising. A department
store in New York wanted to run a special section in their
furnishing department, and they asked me to arrange it; several nightclubs wanted decor; and on many occasions, I was
the commentator for astrologically inspired fashion shows.
My timing mechanism has not yet caught up with itself, although it is on the way, for Sybil Leek watches will be on the
market very soon. I combined forces with a man in Orlando,
Florida, who has a background of many years of merchandising experience. With his wife and my children, we formed
our own company and financed it to produce and distribute
the watches. After all, we all know how successful the Agnew
watch was, and I always wanted to see my face on a watch.

I think I have beaten the old nightmare of being on the
outside and seeing so much astrological merchandising float-
ing around the country. I have nine companies in existence
today, and I do not need any of the six men I met in New
York originally, who did not recognize the practical advantages of my dream. I still have to work out a plan for the
games I invented, but I know they will go into the boiling pot
of my production companies. After waiting so many years to
see my ideas culminate, I have learned the value of patience.

CHAPTER 9

Astrology in the Space Age

Moving to Florida from New York and Los Angeles was an exciting period of my life. I had grown so tired of living in hotels. At one time I loved New York because it was a bright, exciting city, but I always hated the winters there, so I had maintained residences in both New York and Los Angeles.

It was too late to truly appreciate either city. In New York, I witnessed the transmigration of the last shreds of bohemian life from Greenwich Village to the Lower East Side. In Los Angeles, I knew I was about thirty years too late. The glamorous years of the decade before the Second World War would have suited me admirably. I could have loved and identified with the flamboyant stars who created all the glamor that Hollywood was ever to know.

Astrology was booming in Los Angeles, and there were always clients tapping at the door or calling on the phone, asking for horoscopes. One man in particular remains in my mind. He obtained fame as a gentleman's hairdresser and was just in time to cash in on the new trend for styling men's hair instead of just giving a brisk, businesslike crew cut. He earned his second flash of fame by being seen out with numerous starlets, one of whom was to win fame in *The Valley of the Dolls*. Finally, Jay Sebring was to hit the headlines of every paper in the world when he became a victim of Charles Manson and his strange cultist followers in a mass murder that horrified and awakened people to the fact that man's inhumanity to man really knows no bounds, even in a sophisticated society.

Jay used to come to my house on North Manhattan Place when he was depressed, and those occasions grew more frequent as he approached his hour of destiny. The cause of Jay's depression was never constant; sometimes it would be the fear of not having an escort. He seemed inordinately afraid of being alone. Sometimes he would call me in the night just to talk about himself. The idea of death obsessed him, and he was keen to learn all he could about reincarnation.

Gradually he began to be interested in astrology and wanted to learn how to do his own chart. Although he was eager and enthusiastic, he was also an inept student. It was death that intrigued him the most, but only in a very oblique way could this interest be related to his own demise. Over a period of two years, many of his original fears of death were eliminated through our talks. He was a person to whom vacillation came easily, so on some occasions he would say he did not ever want to know the future because he knew he could not cope with the knowledge. The next time he would insist that he wanted to know how long he could live so that he would not let a day go by without appreciating it.

Astrology showed a sudden death for him, but I am thankful that no normal human being could have imagined the horrible manner of death that was to come to Jay. He loved all his friends—not only those who were destined to die with him—and I suppose the terrible desire to relate to people all the time made him seek the company of just about everyone in Hollywood. His success as a hair stylist enabled him to become one of "the beautiful people." Loving the artistic side of life and having a hedonistic longing for luxuries, the horrible manner of his death must have been the price he had to pay for some terrible karmic mistake in a past life.

Poor Jay had to trail his web of destiny from one life to another, only to find death the loneliest thing of all. I hope the price of his karmic debt has been paid fully. In such a way, some of our modern victims live and die with obituaries blazoned across newspapers in every country, and criticisms of their ways of life sometimes obliterate even their shocking deaths.

My astrological life in Hollywood brought me into contact not with the filmstars, but with numerous immigrants from another country. Los Angeles has quite a large White Russian section, and I lived mostly with Russian people. Then a new type of immigrant came along—young, eager to be absorbed into the United States, but bewildered by a country that can be quite autocratic in action although democratic in principle.

One young man who remains in my memory was different from all the others. He was working as a cameraman in a television studio when we first met. I think I was doing a program on astrology at the time, and he came to ask if he could meet me somewhere after the show. It was not convenient at the time, but he came to the house about a week later. He was like a handsome lion, and indeed, he was born with his Sun in Leo. I could imagine him as one of the actors who might have dominated the Hollywood scene thirty years ago. Tall, athletic, good-looking, and intelligent, he had much going for him in a city that thrives on such attributes.

The amazing thing, as I discovered on our first meeting, was that he was homesick. Like many Russians, he was able to cry, which is probably one of the best outlets for pent-up emotions. The British talent for keeping a stiff upper lip under trying circumstances is really no antidote for the inner torment that so many Russians feel and can only learn to live with through the outburst of tears. After such a release, it is always easier for a Russian to talk, and since I have always been a sympathetic earth-mother figure, few men of any age have inhibitions in my presence.

Although Dmitri was certainly not born to peasant stock, he had had a terrible life since he was a child. His grandparents had survived the Revolution of 1917 and believed that the new Russia would be a great country. Dmitri's father lived long enough to express an intelligent disapproval of Stalinism, and he paid for it with years of imprisonment. His family was left to starve and was ill-treated not only by official members of the Stalin group, but by the other people in the little community. Dmitri saw his parents die. His brothers and sisters were left in his care until they disappeared, and then he was left on his own. He remembered that he had promised his father he would leave the country when it became possible. He was twenty-five before the opportunity came for him to join a group of Soviet visitors to Yugoslavia and Italy.

Having defected and reached the United States, he was shocked at the treatment he received when people knew he was Russian. A fugitive from communism who had seen his family wiped out by the regime, he could not understand why so many people viewed him with suspicion. Everyone in just about every sphere of life, professional and social, with-

drew from him and remarked that he was possibly a com-
munist who wanted to infiltrate the United States for devious
reasons. He heard of the White Russian colony in San Francisco and Los Angeles and managed to trek overland to join
them. He had picked up some camera techniques during his
Russian days, when state education was just starting programs and lessons to build up teams of technicians for the
film business. Helped by friendly Russians in Hollywood, he
managed to get a job in the television studios.

When he came to me, he was suffering from the reaction of
being able to compare the easy-going people in Los Angeles
with the more antagonistic ones in New York, but the
amazing thing was that he was also homesick. He had felt an
alien in Russia because of the ideologies, which did not appeal to his intelligent nature, and the bitterness of losing the
father who was, undoubtedly, a great influence in his life. In
the United States he felt a different type of alienation. He
told me he wanted to be Russian and be proud of it; he did
not want to be treated as a leper when his country was mentioned. He knew its faults better than anyone, but love of
country can be a dominant force in many a Leo's life. Now
he was really without a country, and he was reduced to be-
wilderment at the lack of warmth and understanding. Like
many foreigners, he had an image of the typical American,
and then he had to discover that there is really no such thing.

Dmitri, then, was living in a limbo with no identity when I
first met him. Throughout our many talks, and by doing his
horoscope, I had the idea that he should write. He admitted
that he had started a notebook in which he recorded his experiences and emotions. When he defected, he had made his
way to Paris for a little while and had had some weird experiences there. (Anyone who can live in Paris without papers for
eight months must always have a story to tell.) Dmitri had

Mercury in his fourth house, and this generally indicates a retentive memory, pride, and many changes in home life. All these attributes can be useful to a potential writer.

He spoke French very well, had a smattering of German, and was working hard at learning a good, intelligible English. I helped him in this, but the trouble came when he tried to write in English. He could verbally express everything with great beauty and forcefulness to me, but his literary efforts were meaningless. Nevertheless, he had a story to tell and I helped him to work on it.

Finally, a creditable manuscript emerged, a pathetic but beautiful documentary of a young man forced to give up his birthright and seek a new life in a strange country. I submitted it to an editor in New York, who liked the idea but did not have the time to help make the book more readable for the American public. By this time, Dmitri did not want to do any more work on the book, feeling it was to be just another failure in his life. I worked hard at keeping up his morale, helping him with his English and pointing out the good aspects in his horoscope, such as the well-placed Mercury. Then I had to leave Los Angeles and come to Florida, but I managed to extract a promise that he would work on the book.

I had been in Florida for two years when a letter arrived to say the book had been accepted by a major publisher. The letter was stilted and alternately moved from good French to mediocre English, but now there was a new warmth and enthusiasm in the overall tone of the letter. He had something to look forward to, and in the fall of 1971, Dmitri's very personal document of his life will be in print. The latest I have heard is that movie rights are already being negotiated.

As an immigrant myself, I think that the large lady guarding the entrance to New York harbor has once again added another child to gaze in wonder at the torch of freedom she holds forever aloft. "Give me your tired, your poor," is part of the message she has for immigrants. Sometimes the poverty, the needs, and the hunger of the immigrant cannot be assuaged simply by the material things of life, but whatever else is needed to make a man feel complete can also be found in the United States. Writing a book will not make Dmitri a complete American, but many people will begin to see that it is possible to love one's native land, criticize it, leave it, and want to be understood.

I love the Statue of Liberty, but I think only an immigrant coming from a war-torn country, or one radically different from the United States, can really appreciate all that the large guardian of the waters really implies as she gives her Mona Lisa smile to all who pass beneath her. Dmitri has found his personal freedom in the United States; his horoscope shows that he can continue to write for many years. With Mercury, the planet of communication, so well-placed, he had an astrological direction to do so, and his environment and education having been different from anything a native-born American is used to, he may help to establish a much better communication between Russia, his homeland, and the United States, his adopted home.

Julie Meredith, a great folk singer who was beaten to the post in the popularity stakes by Joan Baez, came to live with me for a little while. She had drifted through life for many more years than she likes to remember. After some basic instruction in astrology, she proved to be a fine student and is now well established in her own right in San Francisco. She is also very psychic and has reconciled herself to the fact that she can sing in coffeehouses and enjoy them but lead a much fuller life through astrology and occultism than she might have done if she had achieved all her ambitions to be a great folk singer.

Julie had stars in her eyes when it came to thinking, living, and talking about show business, but she matured enough in the time I knew her to see that it is truly not such a glamorous, fulfilling life as she first imagined. I think she found herself through astrology more than anyone else I have ever known. She has a great voice, a remarkable stage presence, and magnificent talent as a composer, but her main satisfaction comes through her ability to help other people through astrology. She has grown into a warm, wonderful person whose door is always open to others less fortunate. She collects people who need people and becomes a bridge to their material and spiritual lives.

No, Hollywood was not a succession of glamorous stars trekking to my door, although numerous starlets came because they did not have enough money to go to some of the other astrologers, who have made a name for themselves in the city of light. My clients were the eager young creatures who grew up to be "the beautiful people." They got a horoscope from me, but also a bonus of tea and sympathy that was based on realism more than sentimentality. One of the greatest things in my life is to have lived long enough to see people I knew years ago make good in various spheres of life. They may not always end up on Broadway, but they become mature people, capable of extending whatever I can pass on to them. I suppose, in the total assessment of my own very varied life, that I am mainly a teacher. I would rather be this than a famous astrologer and psychic, but I know that astrology and occultism are necessary components to my understanding of others. My astrological clients always seem to come along in specialized groups, and gradually, I think, I shall have had experience in every segment of life, from crowned heads to budding starlets, from politicians to financiers.

Florida proved to be the means of adding yet another group of people to my astrological portfolio. I live some twenty miles from the famous Cape Kennedy, home of the United States space program. When I came to Florida, I did not come to the little township intentionally. I was driving from New York with an engineer friend, whose Karmann Ghia stalled by a causeway linking the mainland with the beaches. Stopping at the gas station, I inquired where we were and discovered it was Indialantic. Then I remembered that friends of mine from Connecticut lived there, so I called them and spent the night at their house. Next morning, I discovered that Indialantic, and adjoining township of Melbourne Beach, reminded me of the French Riviera. I loved the waterways and the palm trees, but at that time I never gave a thought to the space program. Perhaps in middle age it is important to revive the nostalgic memories one has carried for so many years. I had always been looking for a place that reminded me of the Riviera, and I never found it until I came to Indialantic and Melbourne Beach.

I found a magnificent house, built in the colonial style, right on the shores of the Indian River, and I lived there for several years, writing books in a study that had one of the most magnificent views in the whole world. Despite its pollution, the Indian River is glorious; nowhere else can one find such magnificent sunsets. I used to stop work every night just to enjoy the sunset, and I felt more at peace than I had during numerous years of traveling. The sunset was like a great ritual to the Sun god. I used to wait anxiously for it to burgeon into a red mass, filling the horizon and changing the texture of the water. Every night it seemed to pay the supreme sacrifice for all humanity as it sank majestically into the watery tomb of the Indian River. In time, the beautiful house itself had little meaning. Only the view mattered, and I fed my soul on the view, for I was spiritually hungry to get back in tune with nature. Urban life in the United States must always be exciting, but the really meaningful moments are the quiet ones when I feel alone with nature.

Gradually I became acquainted with the Cape and was fascinated by the concept of its work—to put a man into space, and ultimately, to land him on the Moon. Through the help of my old friend, Ann Fague, formerly of Connecticut but now working as social aide in the protocol office of General David Jones at Patrick Air Force Base, I began to meet many people working on the space program. Scientists, engineers, astronauts and their families, all seemed to trek to the house on the river, and I was amazed at how interested everyone was in my kind of scientific astrology.

Then I was invited to give a talk about astrology at one of the monthly luncheons held at the Officers' Club at Patrick Air Force Base. I was amazed at how many people arrived for the luncheon, and I understand I broke a record for attendance. More amazing still were the questions from the enthusiastic audience. Not that everyone was pro-astrology, but to a lecturer, an avid interest is much more satisfying than a mutual admiration society. Many ladies came to me afterward, saying they had questions to ask not for themselves, but about their families.

After this talk, there was a never-ending stream of inquiries about astrology, many of them from men at the Cape whose names later became household words in the space program. Practically all the top brass at the air base also had their horoscopes done, and many predictions on world events were solemnly taken to the base to be locked in one of the many safes where they could be checked at appropriate times. Nothing went into safe custody until it had been acknowledged by an officer. Few of them went into active duty or moved to other headquarters without phoning me to ask how their horoscopes stood. Nearly all the officers insisted on a vow that I would never let their wives know that they had had their horoscopes done. At first I was resentful about giving this vow because it seemed too unnecessary, but when I realized that it eased the situation for many of the men, I gave in. It is not that more women are interested in astrology than men; rather, women are more honest about their interests.

I always have a secret laugh when I am being interviewed on radio and television shows throughout the country (the promotion tours still go on, dragging me reluctantly from the Indian River). The interviewers love to imply that astrology is only for women, lonely people, and anyone who is slightly kookie. Nothing could be farther from the truth of astrology as I know it. Right from my own grass roots, I have always known highly intelligent men and women who were interested in the subject, and many of them were of the professional caliber of H. G. Wells. Of course, astrology also has its antagonists, just as the space program or any scientific venture must. Perhaps the skeptics as well as the adherents act as a catalyst and keep astrology going. Just as I am not an evangelist for witchcraft, so I do not insist that astrology is for everyone. Those who want to study it can do so, and should be free to do so, while those who hate it—generally through lack of understanding—are equally free to do so. It was refreshing, though, to live on the "astronaut trail" and find so many people deeply interested in astrology. I found a new lease on life by doing horoscopes and teaching astrology to the people living and working around the space program.

The preliminary Apollo shots were always highlights of my life, bringing in a great rush of business in personal horoscopes. Through mundane astrology, I could ascertain if such shots

would be successful. The eyes of the world were turned to
Cape Kennedy when Apollo 11 was launched. As a journalist, I
was able to go to the huge press site at the Cape, which was
just about as close as people can get to watch the launchings.
There was no doubt that Apollo 11 would be successful. That
exciting day I did perhaps forty broadcasts from various
broadcasting units at the Cape press site. With my photo-
grapher-son, Julian, I spent a solid twenty-four hours at the
Cape before and after the launch, but we had the comfort of
knowing that all would be well. I never had that fine feeling
again at any other shots.

Many Indian and Japanese broadcasting units were very
seriously interested in the application of astrology to the
space program. The interesting thing to me was that they
accepted the validity of astrology and asked constructive,
intelligent questions. There was no larking about in their
interviews, but the usual top American studios who were
represented at the press site seemed to find it highly amusing
that an astrologer should be interested in a scientific program. I had learned by then that it is not possible to educate
everyone in the broadcasting media, for many were still in
the grips of antediluvian thinking that made astrology suspect
program material. At the time of Apollo 11, the British
Broadcasting Corporation had maintained their taboo on
spiritualism and occultism for many years. It is strange that
the news media, which is concerned with presenting world
events, has ignored a topical subject longer than the man in
the street, who has always been aware that astrology, on one
level or another, plays a vital part in his life.

Apollo 11 was more impressive than any of the other
Apollo flights. When Neil Armstrong spoke his message to the
world—"That's one small step for man, one giant leap for
mankind"—it was applauded by everyone who knew the

space program. It seemed like the end of one of the most enormous projects ever conceived by man, and many compared it to the voyage of Christopher Columbus. Actually it should have been the beginning of a new way of life for the United States as the pioneer of space, but barely had Apollo 11 gone into orbit when the first throes of depression made itself felt in the loss of men who had dedicated twenty-five years to the idea of putting a man on the Moon. The dream of H. G. Wells and my own father was a reality, and I felt privileged to witness it in the company of the greatest newswriters in the world. What an anticlimax all the other launchings were. After Apollo 14, all the glamor and glory was completely gone, and fine engineers were leaving their jobs in the gigantic cutback decreed by Washington. Success in the space program reached a point of never again capturing the imagination of the world. Poor public relations by NASA and the government reduced one of man's greatest achievements merely to being a controversial weapon in the hands of a group of people who saw it as a waste of money.

Astrology keeps up with the times and is of the times, so it is logical to presume that an astrologer can take a group of people, such as the rare breed of astronauts, and discover a specific pattern. In short, there is likely to be a common denominator in all horoscopes studied, and from this common factor, results can be assessed clearly enough for the astrologer to predict success or failure. Every age produces a new series of patterns, and in our age the most exciting one must surely be the trends that make a man into an astronaut.

It is wrong to think that astrology belongs to the past, for it moves with the times and always updates itself. But the updating is only as good as the astrologers of the age, who must look for new patterns in the astrological maze. While we must be faithful to tradition, just as a mathematician or doc-

tor must be faithful to his basic tradition, we must not be
afraid to see the events of our own times reflected in the
mundane and personal horoscopes. Uranus, Neptune, and
Pluto play a great part in establishing new patterns in astrology. Uranus is concerned with electricity and electrifying
changes; Neptune, with new religious feeling, hypnotism,
changing values in spirituality, and scientific discoveries. It is
no coincidence that the discovery of Neptune heralded such
things as the first gas lighting of cities and the first use of
ether in medicine. Many other "gaseous" discoveries have a
direct line of astrological reference to the nebulous planet,
Neptune. Pluto, we know, is concerned with regeneration by
obtaining order through chaos and ultimately rebuilding.

All these features are very much part of our life today; we
are hesitant explorers on the periphery of the Aquarian Age,
which is ruled by Uranus. Finding the new pattern specific to
our age is an intriguing part of the life of the twentieth-
century astrologer. In order to find it, the astrologer must
become a dedicated researcher, delighting in the work itself,
since no one as yet sponsors the thousands of hours of work
necessary to find and establish the new patterns.

It is best to try to get a run of some five hundred charts to
find relationships in a given field. It is easy enough to get the
charts of five hundred families, but not at all simple when it
comes to establishing a pattern in such things as organ transplants in medicine. In the late years of my life, I know I shall
be able to present the world with a complete survey of ten
new patterns in astrology useful to astrologers in the Aquarian Age, but I am only just beyond the halfway mark in my
research. If I could concentrate on nothing but research and
could be sure of having a roof over my head and enough to
eat, I could probably get results in the next seven years. What

should be a full-time job has to be a part-time one for financial reasons.

Of course, there are two areas that fascinate me more than
any others. One is finding new patterns in medicine (which
must obviously be there and known in order that the many
"new" diseases we are subjected to can be understood), and
the other is the space program. Since I live in Florida, the
space program takes precedence over the medical research
because the basic data is more easily available.

This line of research presented a great challenge to me as
an astrologer. I have been interested in space travel ever since
my childhood, when I listened to H. G. Wells and my father
talking about it as if it were going to happen tomorrow. As I
began to do personal horoscopes for people at the Cape, including all the astronauts, they were revealed as some of the
most interesting people of our times. It is strange to think
that what must surely be the most amazing achievement—
putting a man on the Moon—has had such a drab presentation
to the public. Reading any of the magazines and papers, the
astronauts emerge either as rare, godlike creatures unable to
relate to the rest of mankind, or as cardboard characters with
little depth or dimension to them as people. Every chart I did
revealed something about their personalities. Aided by my
son, Julian, who has always been oriented toward the space
program, we began an extensive research project on horoscopes pertaining to everything and everyone at the Cape.

The data for the astronauts was provided by official sources
at the Cape, and we took great pains to discover the birth
times of all of them. When an astronaut did not know his
birth time, we had to do a lot more work rectifying the time
by asking for two specific important events in his life. From
the time and date of a marriage or the death of a parent, we
could work backward through the ephemeris to discover ex-

actly which planets were on the eastern horizon at the time of birth. This is a hard way to work, and it is one of the reasons why most commerical astrologers are reluctant to do a simple natal chart without reference to the time of birth. In scientific astrology, it is most essential to know the time of birth. Even if it takes up a lot more time, it is well worth the effort.

Shortly after midnight one night in the fall of 1968, just before the projected flight of Apollo 11, Julian called me to his workroom. He was very excited, bright-eyed, and full of enthusiasm as he shuffled through a mass of papers on his desk. If he had shouted "Eureka" I would not have been surprised, for he had indeed found a new pattern in the mass of horoscopes he was studying. I could understand his excitement when I began to look at the charts, for the same basic planetary pattern was emerging in all the horoscopes. Uranus in Aries was a constant factor, while Neptune in Virgo was consistent in ninety-seven percent of the horoscopes. A slight variation was apparent when only one degree separated Neptune from moving from Leo into Virgo.

We found that although several astronauts were born in foreign lands and had different places of birth, it made no difference. Uranus in Aries, and Neptune on the cusp of Leo-Virgo or in Virgo, always appeared within 3 to 5 degrees.

The trouble with astrological research is that it never ends. After this, we began a torturous program of doing the horoscopes of all the rival Russian astronauts—where we found the same planetary patterns. It is significant that Uranus should dominate the horoscopes in the pioneer efforts of space travel and exploring new dimensions, for this planet is notably concerned with the exciting scientific discoveries that are taking us into the Age of Aquarius. Uranus is also associated with unexpected dramatic affairs, and what can be more exciting than the idea of man being able to set foot on the Moon?

We were close to the reality of a man on the Moon as we worked on the charts day after day. All those fantastic stories by Jules Verne now seemed to be based more on fact than fiction. An astrologer realizes that only a hair's breadth divides fantasy from reality.

The logical place for Uranus in an astronaut's horoscope has to be Aries, the first sign of the zodiac, whose character is such that it helps men to break into new ventures. It is also significant that Aries is a pioneer sign, whose adventurous subjects can only start work and must leave a legacy for others to continue. They are the trail blazers who must go into action, but they can rarely achieve all that they set out to do in one lifetime. Neptune, the diffuse, mysterious, nebulous planet, seems to indicate the numerous hazards that have already been part of the space program. Dream content is natural to Neptune, and it encourages a pioneer to delve into the unknown and the limitless.

Neptune in Virgo gave me a few headaches to begin with, for I could not quite reconcile the earthiness of the practical, meticulous Virgo characteristics with the romantic excitement of exploring space. The key is probably in the word "practical," more than in "romantic," for in the application of the space program, success depends on a series of specialized operations carried out meticulously with many more hours of preparation, teamwork, and service than people imagine.

In reality, the glamor of the space program is only in the minds of the people looking at it. All the astronauts have a very prosaic, dedicated attitude toward it, which is consistent with the characteristic of Virgo as the sign of service. In order to send a man to the Moon, thousands of unacclaimed men worked with dedication and careful attention to minute details, and all these details are well understood by the astronauts. For them to fail reflects failure on everyone involved in the space program, and no one with strong Virgo trends can bear the idea of letting down his fellow men. The placement of Neptune in Virgo pegs down this deceptive planet, for once, into a place where it can make its most useful contribution. Service and dedication are at their highest point in the lives of all the astronauts, and if we look at the work of past pioneers, we find that few were motivated by monetary or other material awards. The award was always in the success of the enterprise. If death was part of the price, then this type of man was prepared to meet death face to face with stoic resignation.

In the horoscope of the three astronauts who met with the tragic death by fire, Uranus was on the cusp of Pisces and Aries, and Neptune was on the cusp of Leo-Virgo. This leads us to believe that while we now know the planetary pattern for the type of men who become astronauts, we still have to find subsidiary patterns for those who will be ultimately successful. For this, we are using the horoscopes of the three men who made the successful first landing on the Moon, with special reference to that of Sun in Leo, Neil Armstrong, the leader of the expedition.

As we move into the second half of the twentieth century, with every year taking us a step closer to the Age of Aquarius, astrologers will be the first to discover the astrological patterns of many new careers opening up that are indigenous to our age. Astrologers with inner vision as well as mathematical expertise will be the first to appreciate these new fields of research. It is an exciting vision before us, and we shall find astrologers ready to meet the challenge, just as the ancient astrologers met the challenge of astromedicine long before doctors banded together as professional men. The gigantic leap into a way of life in which electronics and computers have their place only paved the way to a rare breed of men, the astronauts. They are prototypes of an advance in science that is already being accepted with ease by children who were not born when the space program was conceived. When we take a well-established career, or a new one, we can always expect to find that specific astrological patterns will emerge, and from these we can foresee trends pertaining to the lives of men and the events in which they will take part.

The ancient astrologers looked for these patterns, found them, and recorded them, so that the foundations of astrology as an aid to understanding the nature of man were laid. When studying horoscopes of people intending to marry, they sought a harmonious relationship between Mars and Venus, as we do today. Searching for basic patterns in medicine, they were able to diagnose diseases and the cycles of health and sickness that would affect a man's life. Today, we have updated this early astrology, keeping pace with all the new trends and techniques in medicine, such as transplant surgery. A great field of research is the study of the horoscopes of the surgeons who perform seemingly impossible feats of surgery, just as patients have remarkable recoveries—always the same basic planetary patterns will be found. From my own files on heart-transplant cases, all patients who have died suddenly, despite tremendous efforts on the part of surgeons and nurses, have been operated on while the Moon was in Leo, and the operation was generally done by a Sun-in-Leo surgeon.

Already I have in my file the planetary patterns of many of the diseases of our age, such as arthritis, cancer, and drug addiction. There is a lot more work to be done. There is a breakthrough, however, in the attitude of many doctors concerning astrologers, especially when they find a science-minded astrologer; soon we can expect much more cooperation from doctors who are also visionaries. I thought this kind of doctor had disappeared from our midst until I began to work with some wonderful doctors in Houston. A whole new vista of astrological research looms up to a world that cannot afford the high incident of sickness still in our affluent, sophisticated society. As usual, it is up to the astrologer to break down the walls of prejudice that divide him from other scientists, but gradually it can be done. Perhaps if just one university in the United States would have the courage to spend a little money on research geared to astrology, we could make a big dent in those frightening walls of ignorance and prejudice, which have always held back scientific ventures.

Fortunately, there are always people like myself, who are prepared to spend their own time and money in research, but this is the hard way to go. Who can blame us if we get tired of battling against ignorance on a personal basis? We need the aid of scientists who are prepared to co-operate instead of seeing all astrologers as demented, irresponsible people. We also need to work with psychologists and parapsychologists and everyone else who is interested in trying to solve the mysteries of the nature of man. In astrology, we have a tool which can be used as a key to unlocking the door guarding man's subconscious and psyche.

CHAPTER

Can You Direct Me to the Witch Doctor?

I have always been interested in making documentary films, so when my old friend Jim Newman called me from Hollywood and asked if I had a good idea for making an unusual documentary, I was delighted.

Kansas City seems to produce a special breed of men. They graduate from this nursery school of television and go out into the broadcasting world to make a name for themselves. During a promotion tour there, I had met Jim in Kansas City, where he was attached to the news department of a television station. After several shows, Jim and I were invited to take part in a séance, which was highly successful. After the séance, we were invited to a magnificent banquet that seemed to have slipped out of another century with its splendid antiques and mountains of flowers, silver, and crystal.

I had my iguana, Mr. Verde-Verdi, traveling with me at the time. He made quite a name for himself on all the shows and was a great stealer of the limelight. Even today I can see the incongruous foot-long iguana deciding that the splendid, massive centerpiece was just the place for him to take a siesta. He ambled delicately along the back of my chair, wove his way through the wonderful table appointments, and finally settled down to making a nest among the flowers. There he remained for the whole evening. Fortunately the host, who had made a name and a fortune for himself as the major producer of candles in the United States, was amused by the situation and acted with kindly tolerance toward Mr. Verde-Verdi.

The iguana proved to be the conversation piece of the evening and led, incidentally, to the first discussions about the film that Jim Newman and I later made. I had found Mr. Verde-Verdi in the Yucatan, where he was suffering the ignobility of being tied to a stake in the marketplace of a small town. He had several companions, and I learned that iguanas were often caught and taken to the market to await a buyer. They were killed eventually and their more succulent parts were eaten. Horrified, I purchased every imprisoned iguana and set them all free on the outskirts of the village. But while all the others quickly scampered away, free again, the one who became known as Mr. Verde-Verdi stayed. He sat back on his tail, gazed up at me, and did not respond to the handclapping or shooing that I hoped would encourage him to run into the undergrowth. Fearing he would again be captured (or was it perhaps something in his eyes?), I had no option but to pick him up, put him in my totebag, where he rested very comfortably, and proceed on my exploration of the Yucatan.

He was still in the totebag when I got on the plane, and he behaved well. He adjusted beautifully to life in a brownstone in New York's once elegant borough of Manhattan. After that, wherever I went, so did Mr. Verde-Verdi, joining my traveling zoo of boas and Siamese cats. He grew fat and confident, loved television, and was probably the most photographed iguana in the world.

When I moved to Florida, he came too. At that time, I had a beautiful colonial house on the banks of the lovely Indian River. One day a newspaperman came for an interview. I opened the front door and heard the latest batch of kittens scampering up the big staircase. The newspaperman appeared somewhat glassy-eyed, and I realized that something was happening behind me that had transfixed and practically immobilized the man. I turned around, and on the stairs behind me was Mr. Verde-Verdi surround by six eight-week-old kittens while Geisha, their mother, was encouraging all her brood to follow her.

The reporter finally grew used to the idea that he was actually seeing a rather large, live iguana frolicking with Siamese kittens, and I believe he based his story around Mr. Verde-Verdi and relegated me to the satellite position in the story. Jim Newman, on the other hand, liked all my pets, and we became very good friends. The phone would ring, and it would be Jim asking what was happening with the Leek family. We also had many discussions about films.

When Jim called me from Hollywood, he was quite excited. He had gotten together a small but adequate amount of money to make a documentary, and we agreed to meet for a further discussion at the halfway point of Houston. I flew to Houston—complete with pets, of course—and we worked out the details of the film to be shot in the Yucatan. The idea was to go in search of a witch doctor I had once met. (Everyone else who makes films about the Yucatan concentrates on the famous Mayan pyramids that were discovered by two scientists who spent time in the Yucatan in search of plants from which to make spearmint. Instead, they unearthed the first pyramid, which was originally thought to be a grass-covered small mountain, although it was well-known that the Yucatan does not really have mountains, but merely a few small foothills.)

We went to see Ed Henderson, who has a small film studio in Houston, and he put together a production team. We fixed the time to go to the Yucatan for April 1969. There were several months to draft out further details, but finally the time came for us all to assemble in Houston and start on what was to be an expedition far more exciting than I originally expected the making of a documentary film to be. Ed had gotten a cameraman from Houston University, also a sound engineer. Jim joined us, and with my younger son Julian, we flew off to Merida.

We thought we had all the necessary permits for filming. At this time the ruling members of the Yucatan were very upset at the exploitation under the guise of filming the pyramids. People were pretending to make films so they could get near the treasure spots, which were yielding up their fabulous pre-Columbian artifacts. At every point we found frustration; no one with a lot of camera equipment was appreciated, and our original permits were considered suspect. Finally, through the help of Sally, a girl working at a travel bureau, we were able to contact the right people and obtain the magical bits of paper that we thought would assure our being able to film wherever we wanted.

Merida itself was a great starting point, as all tourists know, but that city of white buildings, with its magnificent, tree-lined, wide boulevards, was not to be the keystone of our documentary. We got some great market scenes and wandered over the rooftops of the flat buildings to find vultures feeding. We bought leather goods at ridiculously low prices when we photographed a factory. We visited plantations of sisal, which was the principal export of the Yucatan before another weed called marijuana made the world grass-conscious. I talked with many natives about marijuana and I found that most of them smoked it. One told me I could buy it in the market, and I did this quite openly with the cameras following me.

We visited the strange structures of the pyramids with their impossibly tiny, narrow steps climbing toward the heavens. The famous observatory at Chichen Itza fascinated me more than any other place in the world. I became lost in a twilight world of half-trance and half-reality as I thought back to the great days of the Mayans, when the astrologer-priests ruled a great domain, and then mysteriously disappeared. Later on, the research I did in the Yucatan led me to the theory that the lost continent of Atlantis, when it is discovered, must surely be linked with the great temples of the Yucatan. Already there is evidence of an underwater wall off the coast of Bimini in the Bahamas. When permission can finally be obtained to search this area, I think we shall find another Temple of the Turtles, and its dimensions will be exactly the same as the Temple of the Turtles in the Yucatan. We are still a long way from the project, though, as we cannot obtain permission from the Bahamian government to do underwater research as yet.

The calendar of the Mayans is famous and is now reproduced as a tourist gift. Many scholars are doing research on the lost culture of the Mayans, although no one has come up with totally acceptable translations of the glyphs that appear on the massive walls. I recognized many symbols that I understood; some were astrological and related to the elements, while others belonged to the secret symbolism of witchcraft. Never in my life have I been so happy and completely comfortable as I was in the Yucatan, and one day I shall return there to live and carry on my particular line of research.

To use the word "comfortable" now seems mad in retrospect, for we suddenly found ourselves filming in temperatures up to 118 degrees. With this came production trouble: the cameras, although supposedly treated specially for use in hot climates, began to "freeze up" with the heat. Everyone but Julian and I felt the heat and suffered terribly from it; I felt as if I had lived there all my life. There is a lot to be said, also, for the long cotton gowns that I always wear. They are especially good for hot climates, but the men did not have this advantage. They were in agony most nights with sunburn. Filming became increasingly difficult as tempers frayed. The time came to go into the interior as everyone began saying, "Now come on, let's get to the witch doctor." At nights, in a hotel without air-conditioning we would go over the day's work and discuss the next part of the agenda. I knew we had to head to the little village of Noona, and for this we needed a guide.

Tourist guides are easy to find—in fact, there is a pool of them at most hotels. But we found no one wanted to go in search of a witch doctor or to be away from Merida for several nights. Finally, on my way to the leather factory again, I found a young boy who said he had an uncle who spoke a little English and who might take us. He took me to a house on the outskirts of the town, where we had a consultation about price. We haggled and got the price down to a level that did not seem as if we were buying the entire car as well as the guide.

We set out for Noona, and when we arrived, we found a religious parade weaving its way through the streets. It was a fascinating sight, with waving flowers made into banners, and incongruously enough, the music supplied by an antique phonograph tied onto a bicycle. Naturally, it was film-worthy, and we followed the procession to the church.

This was a Mayan parade; not a single face appeared to be Spanish, such as we found in Merida. We talked to hundreds of people, and I got to know many of the villagers, whom I loved for their childishness and their strange pride. In Merida, everyone would say "I am Spanish, not Indian," but in Noona everyone said "I have no Spanish blood; I am Mayan." Within two days, we felt we were in a world totally different from Merida. That lovely city is certainly attractive, but it is people who make me remember a town in any part of the world. Everyone I talked to in fractured Spanish and pidgin English was interested in astrology. I was getting so intrigued with my newfound friends that I was prepared to forget all about the real purpose of our visit, which was to make a film. We did a lot of shooting each day, but the cameramen and Ed were getting restless. "Come on, now, where's the witch doctor?" They wanted an address, and I found it hard to explain that I should have to lead them to the vicinity where I had found Mr. Verde-Verdi on my previous visit.

They began to ask the villagers where they could find a witch doctor, and by now they were willing to settle for *any* witch doctor, my friend or not. The cameramen would come back from their foray into the village shaking their heads in disbelief that witch doctors existed at all, for the only thing they got in reply to their questions was a shrug of the shoulders and a blank look.

One evening I was talking with a group of people, and I kept hearing the word "Ah-men" mentioned; when I asked for a translation, there was a silence for a moment. Then a young Mayan told me it meant "the wise man." Apparently, if you want to find a witch doctor around Noona, you do not ask for one, but simply for the Ah-men, the wise man. I explained that I wanted to go outside the village, indicated the direction, and described my old friend; after some consultation, the young Mayan said he would go with us.

The next morning, we started off and traveled for several slow miles in a car that had seen its best days some twenty years ago. It was worse prepared than we were for a journey along bad roads that had not known the wheels of a car for some years. We stopped at another village for drinks and to buy fruit. Small children began to gang up with us, and one broke away from the group to run down the small street, yelling "The Gringos are here, the Gringos are here!"

Immediately we were mobbed by everyone in the village—not in an unfriendly manner, but with the curiosity of children. Our guide got into a hectic conversation, evidently telling the purpose of the visit. Meanwhile the cameramen stood grimly by, guarding the car and its valuable cameras and equipment from curious fingers and an overenthusiasm to discover exactly what else we were carrying.

The sun got hotter and hotter, and the earth burned through the soles of my sandals. Finally the guide told us we had to leave the car and proceed on foot. There was a good hour's argument over this—the car seemed to represent security to my fellow travelers, and knowing the American's disinclination to walk when he can use wheels, I felt it was not going to be a day when I was likely to be popular. By now we were two days beyond our estimated shooting time, still with no sign of a witch doctor. It was no hardship to me, for I loved everything I saw, but my good sense told me that time is money. Today we had to find the witch doctor; otherwise, *Mutiny on the Bounty* would be reenacted, and I could not see myself in the role of Captain Bligh. Witch doctor or bust was the verdict, and bust we nearly did.

We managed to drive the car a few more miles. Then the

road really ran out on us; there was nothing to do but aban-
don the machine once and for all. Even though we were in an
isolated area, my friends were still worried about the Mexican
habit of stealing things from cars, so we had to take everything with us. Everything! Ed remarked sourly that we had
paid excess baggage rates on five hundred pounds of equipment, and this was what we now had to carry. We each took
something from the car, locked the trunk, and proceeded like
natives on a safari along the travesty of a road. At several
points we had to climb up and around huge boulders, and the
merciless sun beat down on us all the time, making the metal
parts of the equipment heat up and adding to our discomfort.
No one spoke for several miles, until we came to another tiny
village.

This village consisted of a small primitive lane of huts.
Every resident had cows and chickens, and we were besieged
by dozens of children and dogs. The dogs were interesting,
since most of them had strange glyphs painted on them. (I
knew this was a relic from past ages, when the Mayans loved
to put a magical mark on everything they possessed.) Little
girls scurried along, carrying pails of water. We seemed to be
a long way from Merida, which had an aura of sophistication
about it in comparison to our surroundings. The children and
dogs had no intention of leaving us. I suppose I made matters
worse, because in my inevitable totebag I had stocked several
pounds of cookies. The children were hungry and the cookies
were soon devoured. In New York's Central Park one may
feed crumbs to the birds, but in the Yucatan, it is the children who hop around hungry for crumbs.

We kept on walking, stopping occasionally to talk to people who came out of the huts to look at us. There was
nothing of the Spanish influence here: we were among de-
scendants of the ancient Mayan Indians, stocky people who

were really small in stature, bright-eyed, very brown, and agile. Of course, we photographed various things on the way: the children, the beautiful faces of some of the women, and the wizened, sun-dried faces of old men, and sometimes we peeked into the stark interior of one of the huts. Animals of all kinds wandered freely together: a dog and six puppies lay exhausted in the heat with the puppies guzzling away at the teats of their mother, while baby chickens used her body as a diving board to attack insects. Then, as the morning gave way to afternoon, and the heat of the Sun upon the roads did not decrease, I began to realize that we were indeed on the way to the last place where I had seen the witch doctor.

My companions were almost beaten into the hot dry path with exhaustion. I tried to cheer them up by telling them we were within sight of the witch doctor's hut. There it was, at the end of yet another lane—the last house, appropriately enough, on a line of identical huts. In most villages in Europe, the home of a witch is generally the last (or the first) house in any village; I suppose this made for easier meeting places in the old days, but it is true that witches of every age seem to prefer a house situated like this.

We arrived at the last hut only to find it deserted. A neighbor down the lane told us the witch doctor had gone away ten days ago to find herbs. When would he be back? The answer was a shrug of the shoulders and "Maybe tomorrow, maybe next week. Sometimes he is away for a month."

Despair hit my companions. "Never drink the water in Mexico" is an age-old tourist saying, but we were beyond listening. We slid the equipment off our backs and eagerly drank water offered to us by neighbors; for once we did not worry that it might be contaminated. It was one of those times when a civilized person, exhausted and defeated by circumstances, gives up and ceases to worry about anything.

I was restless, but a thought in the back of my head kept telling me to wait because the witch doctor would come. I told my companions this, but they said they just wanted to rest. If he came, he came, but miracles did not happen to people like us. I almost became angry because by now I knew that the witch doctor was near. Then it happened, the very miracle that did not happen to people like us. Way down the lane, where it disappeared into the horizon where the setting sun provided a brilliant dash of color in the background, a tiny figure seemed to be moving toward us.

"It's him!" I said, happy and excited. "It's him!"

"It's a mirage," said Ed Henderson. I started down the lane to meet my old friend, and indeed it was the witch doctor himself.

He was a very tiny, emaciated figure of a man, wearing a sweaty, sodden shirt, old pants, a straw hat on his head, and carrying a paper bag full of herbs. He greeted me affectionately, putting his arm around my waist.

"I came back to see you," he said, and if my companions had heard that, they would never have believed their ears. For hadn't the neighbor said the witch doctor had gone away ten days ago? Ten days ago we were in Houston, planning our trip. How, then, could he have known?

I told him we had traveled a long way to make a record of him forever on film. He was not at all impressed and continued to talk only to me, ignoring my companions, with the exception of Julian. My tall, fair-haired son became a great favorite with everyone he met in the Yucatan, since they seem to like fair-haired young people who obviously have no Spanish lineage in them.

The cameramen now came to life, and under Ed's direction, they began to set up the equipment on the grounds outside the old man's hut while he groaned that the light was

fading. Soon the microphones were switched on and the cameras were rolling. I spread my lovely Thai silk shawl on the
dry ground, and the witch doctor and I sat and talked and
gradually became impervious to the cameras. The old man
was intent on explaining the herbs he had gone to collect. It
transpired that one of his patients in the village was dying of
cancer, but he knew of an herb that would help. So he had
set out on foot for the foothills of Uxmal many miles away,
where this special herb grew. . . .

The children, dogs, and neighbors now kept at a discreet
distance from us, much to the surprise of the cameramen,
who were sure they would have trouble with them when they
started filming. Then the scene was disrupted. A woman
rushed into the compound carrying a child, followed by more
neighbors or relations. The child had a dreadful wound in the
head and was covered with blood.

The old man took the child from the mother, murmured
something to it in Mayan, and put his hand right over the
horrible mess of blood, which was encrusted with insects. He
held it there while we prepared ourselves for the screaming
that we felt should follow. There was nothing but silence, as
if the world stopped for an entire moment of time. When the
old man removed his hand, which was unhygienic by modern
standards, with dirt from the plants ground into the skin, the
bleeding had stopped. He put the child on the ground, and it
toddled to its mother. There was some conversation, and the
people moved away.

The witch doctor sat down again and continued his conversation with me as if nothing had happened. I asked him about
his work. He said he was mostly concerned with healing; he
was midwife to most of the children. No doctor ever came to
the village, and I doubt if the people would have used one,
for primitive people have a distrust of the professional medi-

cal man. The old *brujo* was also a counselor, and he laughed
as he pointed to a few girls in the crowd. "They have troubles
of the heart here," he said.

"Do people come to you when they want a man to love
them?" We laughed a bit; we were united by the age-old practice of people seeking the means to get love, whether it is in
Manhattan or the Yucatan.

We filmed for as long as the light lasted, but while the men
were putting the equipment away, the witch doctor and I
continued to talk. I felt a tremendous warmth toward the old
man. We went into his hut, and there was nothing there but a
cooking pot, a water vessel, and blanket, and a tiny stool. I
picked up the stool and immediately the old man asked me if
I wanted it as a gift. I accepted, but I asked him if he would
keep it for me and use it. The acceptance of the gift was all
that mattered, but I wondered how a man with so little could
dream of giving me one of his very few possessions. I marveled that anyone could live so primitively in the twentieth
century and still be as happy as our witch doctor seemed. In
Africa, huts in townships comparable to this one would always have some form of art work in them, but here there was
nothing. He has nothing to leave behind, I thought remorse-
fully. One day the witch doctor will die, and who will remember him? Nothing to leave a potential heir, nothing to
say a good wise man once lived in the hut and proved his
worth to his small community.

There, of course, lay the answer. Perhaps a man does not
need to leave behind physical things to be remembered. I was
sure the woman with the wounded child would tell many
generations of grandchildren how the local witch doctor
saved his life and stopped the child's lifeblood from running
away. The thought cheered me up. I did not want the witch
doctor to be forgotten any more than I want witchcraft

itself to be forgotten; I know it will always be remembered by those who have been exposed to its practices.

As we left the compound, I gave the witch doctor a large silver Mexican coin. He looked at it with surprise; I suppose it really might have represented wealth to him if he thought in terms of money. But he gently took the large crystal that I always wear, a treasure from my grandmother, fondled it in his grimy hand, then with his other hand held the medallion to his own chest. I knew he was telling me that he regarded the coin as an amulet, a gift in exchange for the stool, and its monetary value was nothing.

I asked him if people paid him for his work. "Not money," he said. "Not many of us have money here, and there are many children to feed." But his neighbors looked after him by bringing him food, and he lacked nothing.

We said good-bye with a degree of reluctance on my part. I would have stayed there for several days had I been on my own, and I would have enjoyed learning more about herbs from the witch doctor. My companions were shocked that I tasted everything he took out of his bag. "This," he would say, "is for the liver, this for the cancer, this for the pain in the back." Some of the herbs were acrid to the tongue. I guess I may have gotten myself nicely doped with all the herbs I sampled; I felt happily light-headed as we started on the gruesome road home. "Home" was actually the car, where we slept solidly that night until the merciless dawn and the blazing sunlight forced our eyelids open to yet another day. We drove back to Noona, stopping awhile to film the big cathedral-like church there, which few people go to, for they prefer the tiny Mayan church around the corner. We finally got back to Merida, the epitome of civilization after what we had gone through. We were glad to sleep in the hotel beds, and even the lack of air-conditioning hardly mattered after the intense heat of the village.

The cameramen were uneasy and were still suffering from the heat when yet another hazard hit them. That night at dinner, everyone felt ill. It was Montezuma's Revenge creeping up on them—the sickness and accompanying diarrhea that spoils the holiday for many people who go to Mexico and the Yucatan. Of course, they blamed the water we drank in the village, but I pointed out that I, too, drank copious amounts of it, and I was not sick at all.

The film company was deteriorating. Even Jim Newman, who had been the most patient during our mad trek to find the witch doctor, was not as cheerful as usual. For twenty-four hours I had the exclusive use of the car because everyone else stayed in bed, so I explored Merida and the surrounding district, thoroughly enjoying it and always feeling that I had been there before. I heard of a nightclub that presented in acting and dancing the many legends of Mayan history. In fact, I kept on finding restaurants that put on similar shows, and I had a fantastic night visiting one after the other. One presented a sophisticated version of the Legend of the Deer, which I remembered seeing at Lincoln Center in New York, given by the Folklorico Dance Company of Mexico City.

Finally, we filmed the most spectacular scene of all: a sacrificial ritual was performed in dance and mime in an impressive subterranean surrounding with a huge underwater lake in the background. The scenes were reenacted in a deep grotto with natural air-conditioning that made it a popular place to visit. The sacrifice was beautifully acted with the high priest, the handmaidens, and the gods attending the sacrifice of a very beautiful young girl. But the high priest had a beard, and

I wondered why someone had not noted in their research that the Mayans have a fear of hair on the face or body? Even with such excellent choreography, a bearded high priest spoiled the whole thing for me, but I do not suppose anyone else noted this small detail. The strange thing is that I was conscious of the beard from the beginning, as the priestly entourage came slowly down the steps into the grotto, and it offended me. Later I confirmed the fact that facial hair was abhorrent and forbidden in ancient times, even before Atlantis sank and the Mayans disappeared from their cities.

The experience in the Yucatan was a satisfying episode in my personal life. I knew we had a good film, but also I had the feeling that I was in the best place in the world. Perhaps in some past life I had been interwoven with the fabric of its history—but these are not the things to talk about to cameramen! On the plane flight to Houston, in the seats around me, the crew talked about the horrors of the expedition, but I felt detached from them. They had not been in my special world, but I hoped that some of my experience of it would come out in the film. I closed my eyes and saw again the appearance of the witch doctor, the glyph-branded dogs, and the eager-faced, laughing children.

When we landed in Houston, I was almost ashamed to hand the crew over to their wives, who immediately noted that their husbands had been sick and had lost weight. On frequent visits since making the film, my Houston friends never cease to talk about the tortuous documentary we made in the Yucatan, but I have my happy memories, which no one can take away.

Several weeks later, however, we ran into financial trouble. There was very little money to take care of editing the film, which is always expensive. Gradually it took shape, though, and we showed the first trailer of it at Bill Graham's Fillmore

East Theater. It had a good review and was praised as the only bright spot in the program. It is now showing in California, but I have still not seen the finished version myself. It was enough to have made the film, found the witch doctor, and proved to skeptics that in the twentieth century such men still exist and are respected in their communities.

I hope the witch doctor sometimes thinks of the strange Americans who visited him. I doubt that this descendant of a once great, proud people, who left behind a culture that we have not yet begun to comprehend, ever wonders about the fact that we recorded him for posterity. When we solve the mysteries of the Yucatan, when we understand the real meaning of the pyramids and their fantastic carvings, maybe we shall find clues to understanding ourselves and knowing that the magic within people can never be destroyed or lost.

Under the blue water of the seas around the Bahama Islands there lies a clue to our own civilization: Atlantis waits to be reborn again in the minds of men who are approaching the Age of Aquarius. The indestructible temple will reveal its own story very soon, but a mess of red tape will have to be cut before we can dive down and see if the measurements of the under-water temple off Bimini do, indeed, match the Yucatan's Temple of the Turtle. What a day that will be, when Atlantis rises again, as the sleeping prophet, Edgar Cayce, predicted. I want to be around when that happens. One of my predictions is that members of my family will be mainly responsible for completing the details of the great expedition that must soon dive into the translucent waters around Bimini.

CHAPTER

A Funny Thing Happened on the Way to an Astrology Forum

Many years ago, I was invited to visit St. Louis, Missouri, to give a lecture at the Theosophical Society Lodge, of which Mr. Charles Luntz is the President. It was the beginning of a long friendship between Charles and myself, and it also brought me in touch with many wonderful people in St. Louis. Jack Samuels, the public relations and advertising man for the lodge, has been in business in St. Louis all his life. He has his finger on the pulse of the tempo of the city, for he was born, went to school, and started his own advertising and publicity business there.

My lecture was a sellout success and helped to put the lodge financially back on its feet. I went back many, many times, always with the same interest, and I made many friends in the town that I grew to love and appreciate.

Charles Luntz is probably one of the best astrologers of

the twentieth century. He was born in Birmingham, England, but he came to the United States and married an American girl, Idelle. Together they worked to make the Theosophical Society of St. Louis one of the most vital lodges in the country. They added a huge auditorium to the mansion, helped to make it free of a mortgage, and they did wonderful work, helping anyone who came to the meetings. I met Charles and Idelle in the twilight of their years; they had already celebrated fifty years of married life.

It was always my dream to start a school of astrology, for I realized I could not do all the teaching by myself. I literally had thousands of requests from all over the United States to personally conduct astrology lessons, but my time was very limited. When I moved to Florida, I wanted to get all my enterprises into my home state. I love Florida for its geographical position, its abundance of water, and the sunshine all through the winter. From a business point of view, though, it presented drawbacks I was never able to overcome. First of all, it has limited television studios and consequently there is little TV work available as a writer or as a personality interviewer. Miami, Orlando, and the west coast regions are far better than my own area, which is ironically in the shadow of the United States space program. I can practically lie in bed and watch our astronauts hurtling into space, but the cutback in the space program is not conducive to businessmen investing money here or to the general business life of the area. Also, when I wrote to the local chamber of commerce and to Tallahassee, the State Capital, for some information about starting several new business enterprises, I was not even accorded the courtesy of a reply.

Ever since the Disney Corporation broke ground near Orlando to put in a Disney World that will be bigger and better than the one in California, everyone on the east coast of Florida has had a dream that the spill-over of people visiting Disney World would flock to the east coast to see the Atlantic. But some months before the official opening of Disney World, no one in Florida had done much to provide amenities for these visitors. True, the Atlantic is there, and it is safe to predict that it will be there for many thousands of years. It seems the local chambers of commerce have little time to spend with would-be individual investors who have time, money, energy, talent, and want to bring their business interests here.

So my idea of a school was stillborn, as far as Florida was concerned, and I left it in the recesses of my mind until I talked again with Jack Samuels, who wanted me to do yet another lecture at the Theosophical Society in St. Louis. Once there, we had the usual wonderful turnout of people, plenty of television and radio promotions to do, and a good welcome from all the newspaper columnists. "Why not start your astrology school here?" said Jack, and from that point on, we were in business.

During his years at the lodge, where he held regular classes in astrology, Charles Luntz had already trained people we could use for instructors. Jack made his offices open for discussion of the school, and the three of us formed Astrology Dynamics Incorporated, a corporation originating in Missouri. We believed that we should consult a professional franchise person about our intentions, and Jack set up an appointment with one. He was charming, had a fine office, an intelligent secretary, made good coffee, and professed to be interested in our project. He thought he could "set up the

whole thing for us"—then came the body blow—"for about
ten thousand dollars to begin with, and a percentage of the
business that ensued."

All we wanted to know was how we could license schools
throughout the United States. We did not feel like handing
out ten thousand dollars in the beginning. So Jack and I
walked to the car very quietly and silently, and without saying a word, he drove to a printer. We got a quote from him
for printing some lessons, paid him a few hundred dollars,
and within a few days we were ready for business. We had an
office, a secretary, six ready and willing instructors, and a lot
of enthusiasm. Jack persuaded all kinds of people in the sub-
urbs of St. Louis to let us have a room for each night of the
week. I went on television and radio and did newspaper interviews to promote the opening of the school.

Meanwhile, Charles Luntz collapsed and was taken to the
hospital, where the doctors were gravely concerned. While
promoting the school, Jack and I managed to pay a daily visit
to the hospital. Charles was so sick on some days that he did
not even know we had been by. The doctors kept shaking
their heads at his rapidly sinking condition. But George
Kayisch, one of our instructors, fortunately knew Mr.
Luntz's horoscope, and from it we saw that Charles would
live. We got him home to the lodge and managed to get people to help look after him, for his wife Idelle was also sick in
the same hospital. Finally we got them both home, and
Charles rallied enough to ask about the school.

The launching of the school was a larger operation than we
thought it would be. Every night I gave a preliminary talk
about astrology. Then anyone who had attended the lecture
could stay on and have a lesson. Enrollments were good, and
it was obvious that St. Louis was astrology-minded. Britt's

stores placed their auditorium at our disposal and gave us some nice publicity by displaying my name and that of Astrology Dynamics on their huge advertising marquee. We met in a lovely little German restaurant in Clayton, well-known for its chess players, where everyone played chess as I spoke. The television camera came in and filmed the lessons and the opening speech. A lot of people enrolled. Next we went to a real estate office, a Holiday Inn, hotels, a steak house, a business training school, a barber shop, an apartment house, and in a beauty shop, with a full house, it was eerie to have an additional audience of wigs on stands all staring with blind eyes in my direction. We seemed to be forever whizzing from place to place, talking about astrology all the time, and every night Jack and I were ready to drop in our tracks from sheer physical exhaustion.

Enrollments rolled into Jack's office. The secretary was kept so busy on the phone answering inquiries that we decided after a month to employ another secretary to deal only with Astrology Dynamics.

The news of the success of the school was better than medicine for Charles, who was directing operations from his bed. He was very much alive and well, and was regretful that he could not get out and give talks himself. Within one month, we knew we had a successful operation, and the school has gone on from success to success. We still have fine, dedicated instructors who firmly adhere to the Leek-Luntz method of teaching astrology.

We decided to add a correspondence course to the school, and we simply used my *Astrology Journal* to advertise. The response was enormous, with replies coming from all over the world. This time we took a vacant office next to Jack's advertising and public relations office, and we employed two students to help dispatch the lessons. Within three months we were solvent and popular. Some people would write to the Better Business Bureau to inquire about us, and we were always given a clean bill for business ethics. The number of instructors was increased after three months, and we added many more classes, so that everyone was working a full five days a week. We circled St. Louis with astrology classes as effectively as our friendly planets circle the heavens.

All the newspaper columnists were marvelous and gave us good coverage, but one of the two newspapers in St. Louis refused to take any advertising for the school, so most of it had to be done by radio and television. Gradually we discovered our best advertising was by word of mouth. Our youngest student was fourteen and our eldest was eighty-four; many husbands and wives came, and we began to get requests to go out and give lessons to special groups. Anywhere we could get fifteen people together we started a class, and miraculously, we had very few dropouts.

The beginners' course consisted of fifteen lessons, the intermediate another fifteen, and the advanced course yet another fifteen. At the end of each course, all the students had an examination, and I advised the teachers to mark strictly, for it would not be wise or reputable to grant students a diploma from Astrology Dynamics unless they attained the standard we expected them to maintain. Some students were a little slower than others, and for these we arranged extra lessons at no further cost, so that no one could say we were exploiting students by marking them down in order to obtain more fees. Charles and I were firm in our intention to turn out good astrologers who could go into the world confident and capable of preparing fine horoscopes. If they wanted to go into business for themselves, we knew they would do well and would earn back more than the money they paid in fees.

There are many astrologers in the United States, but I know from experience that there is a dearth of really well-trained, competent ones, and our aim from the beginning has been to give quality instruction.

In December 1970 we had our first graduation class. Jack booked a huge hall in a hotel, and when I went there, I thought our first graduating students would get lost in the vastness of the room. How were we to fill the place? I wondered, but I should have had more faith in Jack. When people began to arrive, I realized that we could have filled even a larger place. The students brought their relations, friends, and employers with them, and presenting the certificates was a spectacular occasion. They were really glowing with pride when they received their certificates. Practically everyone got up to say that the classes had been one of their greatest experiences.

I got home to Florida after being on the road since September 9th, with several hundred television and radio shows behind me. The children had moved my household effects from Houston back to Florida for I had houses in both Texas and Florida and decided to cut down on my expenses. I could not believe there were no classes to teach, no interviews to do, and I was really back in my own home and could relax. I slept through Christmas day and passed the week before the New Year in a state of collapse. Then the phone rang, and it was Jack Samuels to say the enrollments had started again. We were off to the races, swinging away through what was now a well-worked-out formula for success for an astrology school. Charles was still an invalid, but he was willing to help with office work and special classes to spruce up the instructors.

Early in 1971 we began to have many out-of-state inquiries, asking if we were prepared to license our school. Phyllis Schlemmer of Orlando was chosen as the director of operations in Florida, and we planned a big opening in Orlando as soon as we could make all the necessary arrangements. We arranged for George Kayisch, by then our national chief instructor, to come down to help organize the Florida classes and for Jack to handle the executive aspects.

Phyllis is a remarkable person, a brilliant medium as well as a good businesswoman, with magnificent offices in Orlando that were to be the center of the Florida activities. We planned the same routine of interviews and radio and television appearances for myself, culminating in a talk on astrology open to the public to take place at Parliament House.

Everything was fine until the threats began to arrive at the office. A woman called to say that if we went ahead with the meeting, the place would be bombed. I decided this was not going to be our day for getting blown up, so we had the meeting. The place was packed with a very professional audience that was capable of asking numerous intelligent questions, and it looked like a good launching. Then a telegram was delivered to the office with more threats to bomb us out of existence.

We called Western Union to inquire if they could help us find the sender of the telegram, but to no avail. Finally we called in the sheriff, and we placed the whole matter in his hands. We found out that our friend who was afraid to sign her name had also spent money sending bomb threat telegrams to Parliament House. "It was never like this in St. Louis," said Jack. "How come you still want to live in a state like this?"

I was beginning to wonder the same thing, and I felt an

unusual surge of anger. Phyllis was enthusiastic, though: plenty of people in Orlando were keen to have lessons in astrology, and recruiting and enrollment went as well as it had in Missouri.

Despite threats, we were successfully launched by the end of May 1971. Meanwhile, Phyllis had described psychically what she thought the person looked like who had sent the telegram, even to the weight and height. On the Sunday after the opening of the school, a woman wrote a letter to the editor of the Orlando *Sentinel* condemning witchcraft (which I think she must have confused with astrology). Just as I was reading the letter and feeling angry about its lack of logic, the sheriff informed us that the telegram had been traced to the author of the letter. The sheriff also told Phyllis that her description accurately fitted the lady. Also, it had been a woman's voice that had phoned in the threats to bomb us. We began to put the pieces together.

I really believed 1971 was going to be the year when I would gain a reputation for being tolerant. Telephoning bomb scares and sending threats via Western Union are both illegal. As a tax-paying citizen earning my living legitimately, I am beginning to think that I, too, have some rights, that I should be able to go about my business in peace without being harassed by strangers who do not even trouble to get their facts right. I think I can also claim the right, as set out in the American Constitution, to follow my own religion. I never get witchcraft confused with astrology; one is a religion, the other a science, and this is something the public should know as well.

CHAPTER

The Climate of Hate

Years ago, when I was a child, I used to hear people in our household talking about the United States, and generally the trend of the conversation turned to the fact that the most sensational news seemed to stem from this country. For example, the news of the kidnapping of the baby son of pioneer aviator Charles Lindbergh aroused the anger of the world, especially when the kidnapping turned into a case of murder. As I grew older, I became aware that many celebrities in the United States are often threatened with violence, ranging from the sheerly demented type of threat to threats that seem to have a legitimate grievance against the party concerned. Blackmail, rape, murders, gangsters and celebrities scared for their own lives and that of their families, seemed to be the earliest picture I ever had of the United States.

Until I visited New York (when it was an equal surprise

that the streets were not paved with gold, as well as not being filled with thugs), I had little interest in the United States. It was too removed from Europe historically, culturally, and geographically. My opinion changed, after a grand tour of all the states, and I fell in love with the entire country and marveled at its vastness and the diversities of cultures and characters. My grand tour was in the days when New York to a European meant visits to the theaters on Broadway, shopping in Saks Fifth Avenue, and a visit to Greenwich Village to see how the bohemians lived. New York then was a city to be respected, if not loved, and no one dreamed of such things as garbage strikes and draft-card burnings. My powers of prediction could not foresee the day when I, too, would be subjected to threats, blackmail, extortion, and general intimidation.

Venus squaring Mars is an aspect concerned with outrages and attacks on the lives of famous people. Many people think a celebrity should always appear bright, relaxed, and happy before the public. This is difficult unless one can put away the memory of obscene and threatening phone calls, telegrams, poison pen letters, and sometimes the threat of personal assault.

My first inkling that Americans are not as extroverted and friendly as they are depicted was, appropriately enough, in Massachusetts. I was going to give a lecture outside Boston on a cold, snowy night. As I got out of the car, some members of the community threw stones at me. In those days, I was not annoyed or upset, and quite definitely not worried. I felt that karma would take care of everything, but over the years, the impact of letters, telegrams, and phone calls has hurt me much more than a few stones hitting my back. At least in Massachusetts I could see the enemy, but the unseen intrud-

ers who invade the gardens and yards of my residences from
time to time are of quite a different caliber.

I used to throw poison pen letters away, dismissing them
lightly, as they deserve to be treated. Sometimes I would
marvel that so many people bothered to send letters, varying
from a few lines to several pages, without signing their names.
I was not so conscious that the writers of anonymous letters
are also aware of the law and are clever enough to conceal
their tracks. Often I could psychometrize a letter and see the
terrible distortions in the mind of the writer. There is no
redress, really, for the anonymous letter, and it will, no
doubt, remain one of the major hazards in the life of most
celebrities. I suppose what I really despise the most are the
letters, all too often totally obscene, that are signed "A Christian"; I wonder how such people reconcile themselves to the
Christian teachings of brotherhood and love. Unfortunately,
the turning-the-other-cheek technique suggested in the Bible
seems to be a one-way trend—it is always the innocent party
who turns the other cheek. I only have two cheeks, and both
have taken more than their fair share of Biblical treatment.

I have always known that fear has some strange side effects
on the nature of a person. In my life, I have usually had to
help dispel the fears of others. Even in emergencies and times
of personal stress, a wry sense of humor hits me, so that few
of the people who visit me even know that I fully understand
their fears. I have never been afraid in strange, new parts of
the world, such as Africa, the Yucatan, or the Congo, but in
civilized, sophisticated America I have known the torment of
fear in my existence.

Only the disciplines of my life, taught to me since I was a
child, have enabled me to carry on philosophically, doing my
work, making up charts for clients, and retaining a special

tenderness for mankind when mankind is not in its best form.

As I grow older, I am becoming much less tolerant of these letters and personal insults. I do not intend to develop a persecution complex, but I am doing what I have always preached to other people—facing reality. In the United States, no one can be quite sure who is a friend and who an enemy. I withdraw from the world more and more; today I live the life of a prisoner. Even though the prison is my luxurious home, I have the same trapped feeling that prisoners in penitentiaries must know, even though my bars are an elegant wrought-iron gate that has to be kept locked, and I look out on my world only through the solar bricks of the wall around the house.

My pets—the cats, Chihuahuas, birds, and snakes—are supplemented by a Doberman pinscher guard dog. He rejoices in his name of Habeas Corpus, and he is known to have a mean nature. Haby-Baby does not have to make decisions in his life, such as deciding who is a friend and who is an enemy. His allegiance is to four people: my sons, Stephen and Julian, Julian's wife, Candice, and myself. At times, Stephen swears he is not quite sure that Habeas is totally friendly toward him. Habeas is fearless and strong and moves like a puma. His leaping tactics are symphonies of tensile strength, but I would hate to be in the position to receive the impact of his bone and muscle. He cannot read anonymous letters of course, but he understands that people banging on the gates or trying to get over the walls are not of the same human smell as the four people in his life. I hate to keep a guard dog, but the primeval instinct for survival is now heightened in me as I slip away from middle age.

Survival is not really enough. A house is not a home when it takes on the aura of a prison. Somehow the luxuries of

life—the paintings, antiques, books, and flowers—lose their
past magic, and at the same time the material world is exposed for what it is worth—less than nothing—when peace of
mind is disturbed.

Hostility from an intolerant world is nothing new to an
astrologer, particularly one who is famous in other areas of
life. The subject itself has many enemies, especially among
fundamentalists of religious fervor who see astrology as the
work of the devil and the astrologer as the devil's hand-
maiden. However, hostility is not directed toward me just
because I am an astrologer or because I follow an unorthodox
religion. It comes in dozens of forms, and sometimes stems
from those who have so much hate in themselves that they
must direct some toward another target. The celebrity, always exposed to the public through the mass media, is literally a natural target and is rarely able to strike back.

The worst form of hostility is always from someone who
was friendly before. Perhaps this person becomes jealous and
uses other people to fire the bullets she makes herself. I had
this experience in the spring of 1971, and it all started in a
strange way. At one period of my life in England, I used to
be an efficient, knowledgeable antique dealer, as many people know. While in Florida, I received a phone call from a
Texas lady who has the reputation of being very much a
leader in the social whirl of Houston life. Blonde, good-
looking, born with her Sun in Cancer, she has suffered some
severe setbacks in her life. Her eldest son, a teen-ager, committed suicide by shooting himself, and at the time I knew
her, during my sojourn in Houston, one of her daughters was
suspected of having a brain tumor. I received many lengthy
phone calls when she had no one else to pour out her worries
to, and I always tried conscientiously to help her and boost

her morale on the grim days she took her daughter to the hospital. Understanding her horoscope, I made many allowances for her erratic behavior—such as forgetting to return my phone calls, which were chiefly of a businesslike nature. When I returned to Florida, I invited her to stay at the house, and she forgot to cancel out the arrangements. A Sun in Cancer is a Sun in Cancer, indeed, and she had all the wayward traits of this sign dominated by the Moon.

Then, one day in late March or early April, she called the house to tell me that she had some oriental ivories for sale (more specifically, that a mutual friend had asked her to sell some ivories). The price quoted was two thousand dollars. I felt this was too much, and asked her to put in an offer of twelve hundred. Before she put in the offer, I asked her if she wanted to go fifty-fifty on the purchase of the ivories, but she said she did not have any money and, indeed, was desperately embarrassed financially.

In antique-dealing circles it is very usual to give a "fixer's fee" for antiques that are purchased through another person, as opposed to a direct seller-to-buyer sale. It is like paying for information leading to a purchase. This is automatically accepted as anticipating a quick resale of the goods. I sent off the check, and within a day or two, my son Stephen brought the ivories from Houston to Florida. They were disappointing—not as old as I thought they would be, and some blatantly displayed a "made in Hong Kong" label. I had bought them sight unseen, though, and had only myself to blame.

I tried to sell them to three local dealers, but was not surprised that they turned their backs on the netsukes of 1900 vintage. Of course, they could not compare with the larger, older pieces. At least they were attractive enough to be conversation pieces in the house, so I reconciled myself to being the custodian of several bastard netsukes. My house in Florida is large enough to absorb many antiques, and I was not worried about the investment of money, since two of the visiting antique dealers had bought other things, even though they turned down the ivories.

Some eight weeks later the phone rang, and a male voice said very aggressively that I had to return the ivories to my Houston friend. If there is anything guaranteed to make me obstinate, it is to have a strange male voice dictating what I have to do with my own things. I gathered that the male was now her lover, living with her and with a view to getting married. A fleeting memory of her horoscope made me give a wry grimace to myself and chalk up another mistake in the tangled mess of the lady's life.

The gentleman was a former baseball player who took some pride in telling me how tough he was and how many friends he had in the Mafia. I kept my temper very well, but after thirty minutes of tirade on his part, I hung up on him. The entire telephone conversation was recorded by my electronically gifted son, and on the playback, I was amazed at the ferocity and the dangerous overtones. Even then, I felt more sorrow for her than for the insults he had heaped on me.

A few days later, he called again to announce that he was flying from Houston to pick up "his ivories." Still feeling more amused than truly aggravated, I informed him that it would be a useless journey, as I was due to be out of town to open our new astrology school in Orlando. Life was pretty hectic when I went to Orlando, one of the fairest towns in Florida. While there, we received a phone call saying that someone had the intention of blowing up the office of Mrs. Phyllis Schlemmer, our school director. Almost before we had finished laughing, we received several more phone calls. One begged us almost tearfully to forego "our wicked ways," and another asked if we had bathed in the blood of the Lamb.

The lecture to initiate the opening of the school went off successfully, with a full complement of people packed in Parliament House. The gracious, intelligent questions from professional people made the bomb threat seem like a dream, and I never once thought about the ex-baseball player with the yen for ivories. The next day a telegram was delivered from Western Union: "PREDICT YOU EXPOSE WITCH SYBIL LEEK AS SATANIC OTHERWISE BLOOD WILL BE ON YOUR HANDS." It was signed "UNSIGNED."

A courteous request to Western Union to furnish us with details about the sender was met with some very unbusiness-like remarks from the young lady at the local office. We called the sheriff, and he sent a man there who took a dim view of the uncooperative nature of the Western Union employee. (I well remember the day when Western Union would not accept a telegram from me because I wanted to sign it "your fun-loving playmate." It was an in-joke sort of birthday greeting to my old friend, Gene Lundholm of Superior, Wisconsin. The girl was firm: "no name, no send.")

Arriving home, tired but happy about the successful launching of the Orlando School of Astrology, I was surprised when the phone rang at 2:30 A.M. It was my unfriendly ex-baseball player, full of wrath and threats. This time, though, he was directing his attack and threats toward my children, especially Julian. This is a vulnerable area, and in his crude way, he knew it. I let him rave on so that I could record his awful threats, which included a threat to wipe out

the entire Leek family. No doubt he was once a fearless baseball player, but in the case of these threats, he was prepared
to let me know he had "friends in Miami who would wipe
[us] out." He also said he did not have much money, but his
Mafia friends thought so highly of him that they would do
the job reasonably. This sounds humorous in retrospect, but
at the time it made me cold with horror to think that such a
thing could happen in the United States. As he continued his
tirade, my horror gave place to wrath. I informed the police,
and they were marvelous; they patrolled the area around the
house every fifteen minutes.

The night had hardly begun, though, in its nightmarish
quality. The telephone continued to ring every twenty
minutes; sometimes I answered it just to get the recordings
but mostly I let it ring. The last phone call came as dawn
streaked across the sky, and it was obvious that the ex-baseball player was certainly not in training for any physical
event. His voice was slurred with drink, but he was still
aggressive and had invented a few more threats.

The police were again alerted, for I gathered in the last
phone call that he was not making his calls from Houston.
Indeed, he had arrived in Vero Beach, a delightful ocean resort some twenty miles down the coast from my house. He
informed me that he knew where we lived, and Julian was the
one to be "got at first." I began to think of my daughter-in-
law, newly married, and I shivered to think how sad it was
that she should be exposed to the hazards of being a member
of the Leek family. It cheered me up a bit to remember that
despite being as delicate as a piece of Dresden china, Candice
Leek is a crack shot with just about any firearm. For several
days we all slept with our guns loaded and cocked and our

ears listening for strange sounds. Even the Siamese cats, doing
their nightly prowl from room to room, almost made us trig-
ger-happy.

The dangerous Venus-squaring-Mars aspect was moving
into position, and here we all were, alternately seeing ourselves as targets and marksmen. For a peace-loving woman,
this is no way to live. I hate and despise guns and bitterly
blamed myself for having one in the house, but an old news-
paper-reporter friend had given me a derringer as a present a
long time ago, begging me to keep it in case of an emergency.
Somehow I had never thought of violence entering my own
household, although I had seen plenty of it in my travels:
riots in America, war-time atrocities in England, Gestapo
jack-boot kicking in Germany, strange police techniques in
Los Angeles, and husbands and wives scrapping in predivorce
proceedings. If this crisis was to be the end of thirty years of
dedication, at least my last good deed had been done to help
less fortunate people than myself. This was bad thinking, but
it shows the state to which a person sinks when subjected to
a constant barrage of threats. It also revealed my vulnerability in the fact that I had a deep desire to revert to using
black magic even though I despise such methods of escaping
from an upsetting situation such as I found myself in. Yet I
have to admit that it always lurks in my mind as a last re-
source and this is not an easy thing to admit. I dismissed the
idea almost as soon as it was born and reverted to constructive meditation instead of destructive practicality. This was
just another trial by fire such as Aleister Crowley always envisioned. He had fallen by the wayside and given in to such
temptations, thereby making himself much more vulnerable
to evil later on in his life. I had to keep this thought foremost
in my mind although it was hard to do so. I shudder now to

think of this moment of weakness because I know that in all things good MUST and does overcome evil. The most positive thing which has come from this dreadful period of my life is to see it as an experience from which I have learned to be more careful in discerning friends from acquaintances. I had had past experiences in knowing that women born with the Sun in Cancer have the power to cause chaos in my life yet I have constantly bent a sympathetic ear in their direction and suffered from it. This had to be the last time.

I am rather amused these days to find myself walking around with keys in my pocketbook, for I never had a key to any door before. It is not so much a lack of faith in humanity that has me carrying keys now as the necessity to get adequate insurance coverage and cut down the overhead expenses of running a household.

My own adventure into the twilight land of personal fears for the safety of my family ended with a fairly rare aspect known to astrologers. May 31, 1971, saw the Moon parallel Pluto, Venus, and Mercury. These aspects occurred respectively at 6:31 A.M. (Pluto), 2:13 P.M. (Venus), and 3:58 P.M. (Mercury) at Eastern Standard Time. It is considered to be equivalent to the difficult aspect of a conjunction, with the worst parts more emphatic than usual. The three planets involved with the Moon in this tripartite aspect are known to influence small objects, communications, intellect, and analysis, all under the rulership of Mercury. Relationships with crowds, public opinion, wealth from others, and conflict between generations come under the rulership of the Plutonian part of the aspect. Love, beauty, cosmetics, and the decorative arts come under the rulership of Venus.

When this aspect occurred, Pluto was in Virgo, the sign of hospitals, schools, and employee-employer relationships.

Venus and Mercury were both in Taurus, the sign of earnings, possessions, landholdings, banking, and the police as guardians of these matters. The Moon was in Leo, affecting creativity in general, and children.

Every part of the influence of this aspect affected my own life. "Direct communication with the public" was obviously altered! I had to have an electronic monitoring system for telephone calls installed in the house in order to cut down on the direct threats. "Small objects" were the cause of the breakdown in communications—in my case, the ill-fated ivories. My children were affected, as indicated by the Moon in Leo, and there was a break in the generation gap as the ex-baseball player, a man in his early forties, directed most of his threats to me through the vulnerability of my children. My earnings were affected because this period was not conducive to my profession as a writer. The planet Pluto, associated with unexpected and often dramatic and drastic actions, was in Virgo, the Sun sign of both my sons. My own natal Moon is also in Virgo, and the police certainly became the guardians of the entire Leek family, doing a remarkably good and efficient job in providing around-the-clock supervision of the house and land.

The Moon parallel to Pluto, Venus, and Mercury presented a highly complex set of aspects, and also reflected itself in matters of national importance. The aspect is known to affect mass murders, labor-management relations, and student-faculty conflicts. In a small town in California over twenty middle-aged men were found murdered in a field, all of them migrant farm workers, and the manager of the labor force was indicted for the crime, thus fulfilling the labor-management influence, as well as revealing a crime that shocked the whole world.

On the weekend of May 30, I was due to attend the American Booksellers Association convention in Boston. I was unable to go, as it would have involved notifying the police in Boston that I was under attack from a paranoid ex-baseball player, and it was easier for the local Indialantic police to provide protection for the whole family rather than break us up into smaller groups.

One of my favorite editors called to check on the arrangements for my appearance at the convention and was shocked to hear that we were living under a state of siege. There was a moment of silence on the line. Then my editor's gentle voice said, "Sybil, I think you retired too soon from studying black magic. This looks like a case where a revision course could be effectively used and could save us all a lot of trouble."

We laughed, but I think perhaps he had a valid point. I was reminded of my old days, when I lived with a tribe of gypsies in the New Forest. The Evil Eye is never thrown around lightly and is used for the greater good of the whole, meaning, in the case of the gypsies, for the greater good of the tribe. Well, a family is a small tribe, isn't it?

I do not recollect that I made a memo on my shopping list to include black candles, long pins, and children's clay, but it could easily have happened. Astrologers have rights, too.

CHAPTER **13**

The Misunderstood Science

I can understand criticism of religion; indeed, I have had plenty of experience as the target of such attacks. But despite its increase in popularity, astrology is still subjected to a barrage of abuse that seems to be quite unjustified. It would be refreshing to find an attack on astrology based on a knowledge of even the rudiments of the subject. Instead, the attackers seem to rely on a weird array of distorted information, such as thinking astrology is a religion in itself, or that the vast amount of data needed to prepare a horoscope comes from a gigantic flash of extrasensory perception. But then, many people think that yoga is a religion, too, and no astrologer can educate the entire public in one lifetime.

I think that people doing interviews for newspapers and other media communications should at least do some homework on the subjects about which they are interviewing. Of course, the biggest mix-up is in confusing astrology, a science, with mysticism, psychic phenomena, and occultism, all of which are admirable in their own way, but they are not necessarily the major attributes of a good astrologer.

This confused type of thinking is similar to the idea that a fine surgeon must be a man of God and must go to an orthodox church every Sunday in order to retain his skill as a surgeon. As we move into the Age of Aquarius, there is a dramatic last-ditch stand to make orthodox religion responsible for everything that happens. When Apollo 13 ran into trouble and was brought safely back to earth by the combined skill and technical knowledge of hundreds of men in Houston, I was amazed how many religious leaders claimed that it was the hidden hand of God performing a modern miracle. It was certainly a miracle, but it was brought about by the technical know-how of men handling computers. If God was concerned with bringing the astronauts safely back to their native earth, then perhaps He also was responsible for the original accident to the lunar vehicle. I doubt if we can go much longer thinking that God is responsible for all the better things of life but is absolved from such affairs as Hiroshima. We may well begin to ask who guided the hand of the bomber pilot to press the fatal button and unleash a new horror on the world. Of course, this brings us into the realm of the tremendous conflicts we are experiencing today. Youth begins to ask its questions, and when it does not receive answers from the older generation, it begins to put its own connotations upon the meaning of religion. Ultimately, I think, we shall begin to see that God is in everyone and is not an isolated deity giving out punishments to some and accolades to others. Astrology may be the one sane form of reason left in an insecure world that is unsure of itself and religion as a whole. Certainly we cannot emerge into this highly scientific age without some revision of philosophies and religions. Naturally we shall not kill our sacred cows easily and without personal anguish, but the time is right to get things into perspective so that we begin to see science as a whole new way of life in itself. True, it is first a discipline, but we are living in an age when spiritual and social areas are likely to be subjected to the disciplines of science. Already we have a battle being fought about the true nature of the Book of Genesis. To believe this does not mean that individual spirituality will be killed; rather, it means that we may in time come to terms with what the Sermon on the Mount really means. In time, astrology will help man to become less of a hypocrite, since it is a science based on the purity of mathematics and is designed to help us see ourselves as we really are, not as we think we are.

I have never resented criticism from my peers, but I certainly get tired of criticism based on a complete lack of information. If I dislike anything enough, I can either ignore it (which I think would be foolish), or I can seek more information about it in order to present my own case. For instance, I feel I can criticize satanism and black magic well since I have studied both subjects and have weighed them in relation to other things. I can understand the lack of information on the Old Religion, more commonly called witchcraft, because it is still a secret society, but this is not the case with astrology. The information is there for those who wish to study it, and there is certainly nothing secret about it. A wide range of data is available in most libraries of the world, ranging from ancient manuscripts to a full complement of modern-day literature. The worst that one can say about studying astrology is that it is time-consuming, as all sciences are. Think how long it takes for a man to study medicine before he can work with the public. People understand that modern medicine is not evil, and one does not have to be a thoroughly trained expert to acknowledge this. The same should apply to astrology. The tools to destroy ignorance are available in books, so why not use them? With knowledge, criticism becomes valid.

Hand in hand with the criticism of the science goes criticism of the practitioner. Speaking from my own experience, which has brought me in touch with astrologers all over the world, I have never found a corrupt astrologer. Quite the contrary, in fact—all astrologers seem to have a genuine interest in their clients, and the time they spend with them goes far beyond doing the horoscope. A fee of fifty to one hundred dollars is charged to set up a good, detailed horoscope, although it may take up to thirty hours to do. It certainly cannot be construed as an overpaid job. Few astrologers finish with a client once the chart is done and delivered; there are often many consultations, and it is not unusual for the phone to ring a year after the horoscope has been prepared, when a client finally gets around to asking questions. This is about the only professional business that gives such thorough, long-term help. If you go to a doctor, dentist, or lawyer, you are always charged for each visit, and there are additional expenses. I firmly believe that there has to be a spark of dedication and a genuine love of humanity in all astrologers, and it is not unusual for sincere, long-term friendships to occur in an astrologer-client relationship which goes far beyond any monetary consideration.

Some clients are very demanding, of course, and here I
find another parallel between astrologers and doctors. I had
one client in Los Angeles who called me every day for a
month to ask about herself. After preparing the horoscope,
which I believed I had interpreted in clear, straightforward
language, she subjected me to a constant quiz about numerous small details. What she needed was not only a horoscope,
but a shoulder to weep on, and I am afraid she saw her astrologer as a cheaper means of getting attention than a psychologist. The modern astrologer needs to be a psychologist and
must always know how far he can allow the client to use him
and his profession as a crutch. The successful situation, of
course, is when the client sees the horoscope simply as a tool,
and does not think that she can blame the planets for every
tiny thing that happens to her.

I suppose the worst criticism, and the least called for,
comes from a few medical scientists who use arguments
that are no longer scientifically valid and are unworthy of
their own status in the world of science. But scientists generally love to argue, and it is rare that a group of scientists is in
complete accord, even when talking about their own field. I
always wonder why some scientists are so reluctant to study
astrology, yet are so ardent in refuting it. For instance, if
they feel it is a superstition, long dead and buried, why
bother to bring it up so frequently? If it is nonsense, then
someone should examine it thoroughly and come up with a
valid thesis against it. I defy any thinking person to study
astrology seriously for a year and still maintain that it is not
valid. Astrology is based on the laws of the universe that are
the very laws of all science, of action and reaction, and of
cause and effect.

Sometimes astronomers and scientists make dogmatic statements in print that "they have never discovered any truth in the claims of astrology." What they probably mean is that they have not taken the trouble to study it other than simply reading a three-line version of Sun-sign astrology in their local newspaper. Such dogmatic statements should really open up a whole forum in which the scientist should truthfully answer the question "Have you ever studied astrology?" I can only presume that fear is the basis of all such statements. Why do people become illogical and emotional when they speak of astrology? Are they afraid we may all regress into a primitive state in which their work may not be justified or appreciated? Are they afraid that astrology may be opening doors to new scientific discoveries and new dimensions of reality and may upset their status quo? Of course, anything written in a controversial vein about astrology generally hits the headlines, but it is the idea of the controversy, not the validity of an argument, that really makes news. In 1970, *Astrology 14* was hailed as the brightest, newest thing in astrology because the writer tried to prove that we should now have fourteen signs of the zodiac instead of twelve. He based his idea on the precession of the equinoxes (the change in the movement of the stars over the past two thousand years). As the change is infinitely remote, there does not really seem to be enough evidence to base a book upon, much less demand acceptance that the constellations Cetus the Whale and Ophiuchus the Serpent-Slayer should be slipped into the zodiac. However, it is fodder for thought, and at least shows that the writer has some basic knowledge of astrology. He is not presenting a controversial new theory without some pertinent study of the subject. My own opinion is that he is perhaps two thousand years wrong in his calculations and should try again, but I welcome the book as yet another fascinating contribution to astrology.

That astrology has an increasing appeal goes without saying, but it is also sneaking back to the realms of true scientific adventure. Many other professional men are using it as the tool it undoubtedly is. Dr. Edwin Andrews, a Florida ear, nose, and throat specialist, has studied more than a thousand tonsillectomies, and he found the tendency to postoperative hemorrhages occurring between the Moon's first and third quarters in eighty percent of his cases. He found there was little or no literature on lunar folklore. Many of his colleagues condemned his research, but none were willing to test his theories. Nevertheless, Dr. Andrews persevered and wrote about his researches in *The Journal of the Florida Medical Association,* XLVI (May 1960), 1362-66.

Since then, various studies have been conducted to show that the metabolic rate of plants and animals have a correlation to the solar and lunar cycles. This is pure astrological data and doctrine and clearly indicates that all forms of life on earth respond to the cycles of the Sun and Moon. John Nelson of RCA made the news headlines when he predicted electromagnetic storms in the ionosphere for many years and then acknowledged that he based his forecasts on planetary aspects, using both heliocentric and geocentric longitudes. Astrology seems to be coming to a full circle. It grew in importance in the Ptolemaic theories; it fell into academic and scientific disrepute at the time of the Copernican revolution, when it was labelled a superstition or even a heresy, as the orthodox churches berated it as a form of prediction; and now, astrology is returning to a position of repute.

Over one hundred years ago, the scientist Thomas H. Hux-

ley fought for the acceptance of Charles Darwin's revolution-
ary theories about evolution. Huxley said that all new scientific truths begin as heresy, graduate to being orthodox,
and go back again to a form of superstition. History proves
this: astrology has adequately fulfilled Huxley's premise, and
is about to move again from being superstition to being a
full-fledged heresy. Modern fundamentalists, such as Carl
McIntyre, thunder against astrology, and ladies in Florida
write to local newspapers in order to link astrology with
satanism and witchcraft. It's cheerful to realize that the next
logical step must be for astrology to become a totally acceptable science again—and this will, indeed, be the case as we
move into the Age of Aquarius.

While we all know the damage done by auto accidents,
not too many people are aware of the high cost of earthquakes. Often it is a miracle that the death rate is not higher;
only the diligence and tenacity of the population in a strick-
en area keeps the casualties low during great emergencies.
The shock and the aftereffects of an earthquake can be just
as devastating as the actual explosion, and it often takes people the rest of their lives to build up their energies to provide
a new home and rehabilitate themselves. Government funds
are generally available for major catastrophes, but this can be
little consolation. Earthquakes become more dangerous every
year, as more of the earth is becoming inhabited as a result of
the population explosion. Even a hundred years ago, an
earthquake could almost be discounted as a major killer, but
today one could easily destroy a township of one hundred
thousand people. Recently a U.S. government panel recommended a ten-year study to try to estimate where and when
earthquakes are likely to occur. The cost of this program is in

the region of forty-eight million dollars. Similar research programs are being conducted in Japan and Russia. It is a sad thing that not one astrologer has been asked to take part in these programs, since eclipses and earthquakes are very much part of the life work of any scientifically minded astrologer.

We know that earthquakes occur in two well-defined zones: one is the Circum-Pacific Zone, running along the Pacific coast of the American and Asian land masses, and the second runs through the Mediterranean, taking in Turkey and the Pyrenees, through the Middle East, skirting northern India, and passing through southern China to join the Pacific Zone. We know the areas scientifically, but we still do not know exactly when and where earthquakes will happen.

Scientists now know that before an earthquake happens, certain subtle but well-defined changes take place. The sea level may drop by several inches, strain meters may detect tension in the ground, and seismometers may register microshocks indicative of the great power that may rip open the earth. Magnetometers can detect magnetic changes showing that rocks are preparing themselves for a major catastrophe.

All this requires expensive instruments, salaries for technicians, and a great, time-consuming compilation of data. Eight astrologers, given nothing more than three years of time and their own capability to make calculations, could produce accurate predictions of when and where earthquakes will occur. The omission of astrologers from research programs on earthquakes is another example of the bigotry of scientists who must do things their own way, often causing a greater burden of taxation on the people of the countries in which they work. The annoying thing is that the astrologers could predict that earthquakes but would have little idea how to prevent them—scientists would be able to direct their attentions to this enormous task. The prevention of great losses of life could be another area for redirected scientific effort. Towns should not be built in known earthquake areas, and the people already in these areas should be warned in time to make adequate preparations for evacuation. Cooperation between scientists and astrologers could only be beneficial in understanding earthquakes.

Earthquakes do much more than shake the earth. For example, the Agadir earthquake produced huge waves in the Mediterranean that completely destroyed the port of Agadir. These tidal waves, which some scientists say have nothing to do with the tides, are caused when earthquakes occur under the ocean bed. At this point the astrologer will not agree and will find in his charts certain patterns of the Moon in conflict with certain planets, and the Moon, as we know, rules tides. It seems logical to presume that tide cycles have a bearing on the side effects of an earthquake. Indian astrologers have done some remarkably good research on these cycles.

The prediction of earthquakes has always been a major part of astrologers' work, so there is nothing novel about the idea of introducing astrologers to the research committee presently working on earthquakes in the United States. It might even be an excellent idea to train several scientists to understand astrology as an additional means of extending their knowledge—again, this would not be anything new. An ancient scientist called Anaximander erected the first astronomical observatory in Lacedaemon, Greece. He predicted the earthquakes that ultimately destroyed the city, making use of scientific, astronomical, and astrological data.

Another Greek, an important astrologer called Democritus, conceived the idea of atomic energy and predicted accurately the times and places of several earthquakes. It is interesting to note that it took scientists some two thousand years to prove that Democritus had advanced the correct explanation for the whiteness of the Milky Way and the fact that additional planets existed beyond Saturn. Now that we know of Uranus lurking behind Saturn, the work of the astrologer in predicting earthquakes is made much easier.

Dr. Rudolf Tomaschek of the University of Munich, Germany, checked the position of all planets during 134 major earthquakes and discovered that Uranus was always close to the Midheaven position at the times and places where the disasters occurred. Twenty-three earthquakes during the period of 1903-1909 showed that Uranus was directly overhead at the time of the explosion. During these six years, the slow-moving planets, Neptune and Pluto, were in opposition to Uranus.

Uranus, Neptune, and Pluto are known by astrologers to have explosive qualities. A reliable rule for predicting earthquakes is that they always closely follow a solar eclipse and coincide with major planetary conjunctions, both of which set up powerful magnetic fields in space. These magnetic fields are then triggered by the effect of future planetary patterns seen in the transits of the planets at this point. So it is necessary to progress a chart from the time of a known solar eclipse in constellations ruled by Neptune, Uranus and Pluto.

Once the planetary patterns are established, there is a period of expectancy. It takes a series of critical planetary aspects to bombard the magnetic fields and thereby start the seismic shocks. The inching together of the celestial bodies at eclipse time sets up highly intensified magnetic fields in a specific area of space. Meanwhile, other planets are building up their patterns, which will move into the eclipse path. When the two patterns are superimposed, the effect is rather like pressing the button to set off a charge of atomic energy.

An astrologer-meteorologist, George McCormack, was able to predict the Long Beach, California, earthquake that took place on March 10, 1933, basing his calculations on the eclipse of August 31, 1932. Seven months before the eclipse was due, McCormack decided to experiment with the theory that the Sun-Moon-Neptune-Jupiter conjunction could result in an earthquake. The important thing was to find the exact time.

At the time of the eclipse, Neptune would be in conjunction with the Sun and Moon. Neptune, a planet of large mass, would also be close to conjunction with Jupiter, the planet of the largest mass. He found the eclipse itself would occur at 158 degrees of celestial longitude. Consider the circle of 360 degrees and remember that each sign of the zodiac accounts for 30 degrees, and it is a simple calculation to find that the eclipse would take place at 8 degrees of the sign of Leo, which is ruled by the Sun.

Mars is considered to be an energizing planet of the zodiacal scheme and a great catalyst. McCormack noted that Mars would be orbiting close to conjunction of the area of 8 degrees in Leo between March 8 and 12, 1933, seven months after the eclipse. The path of the eclipse fell directly over the longitude of Los Angeles at the moment of totality, so Los Angeles would be the area for a future seismic action.

On March 10, 1933, at 5:54 P.M., Mars was within 1 degree of the previous eclipse area, 158 degrees from Aries. The Moon approached within 2 degrees of the conjunction with Mars. The slowly moving Neptune was still at 158 degrees when the earthquake struck Long Beach, registering

nine on the modified Mercalli intensity scale of twelve. A
thousand people were injured, 115 killed, and the damage
estimated at fifty million dollars.

The planet Neptune is greatly in evidence in atmospheric
conditions of a depressing nature; even its mythology claims
that it has a lot to do with earthquakes. It is, as we know, an
insidious planet, often hiding as it does, physically, behind
something else before making its presence felt. A study of
this history of earthquakes shows that they have happened
at, or immediately after, conjunctions or oppositions of
Uranus, Mars, and Neptune. An entire book could be devoted
to taking all the major earthquakes and showing the corresponding planetary positions together with astrological inter-
pretations. This factual evidence should be placed before the
research committee of scientists now working on the study of
earthquakes. When Saturn is directly beneath the earth at the
point of observation during the times the Sun is at the equinoxes or solstices, the point becomes significant in locating
seismic eruption areas of the future. This position of Saturn
always shows the point of least resistance on the earth and
where the most damage can be anticipated.

A conjunction of Jupiter and Mars influences the earth by
expansion. Jupiter has expansion as one of its astrological
characteristics. We choose to see Jupiter as a benevolent
planet because of these expansive qualities, but we should
not forget that expansion can also increase the propensity for
bad health or earthquakes. Saturn, the planet associated with
restrictive qualities, works in exactly the opposite way of
Jupiter, for it contracts. Finally, Uranus explodes suddenly.
Where an earthquake is influenced by Jupiter or Saturn, the
disaster would be preceded by warnings, such as rumbling in

the earth or minor tremors. The Uranus type of earthquake strikes without warning.

The astrological timing of earthquakes is related to eclipses, conjunctions, and the planetary patterns formed at the time of seasonal change, such as at the equinoxes or solstices. The celestial patterns are formed a long time before an earthquake happens, and it is these past patterns that have to be studied before the future time of an earthquake can be calculated. I see the building up of planetary patterns rather like the nerves that send messages to the brain which trigger future action.

By the time this book appears in print, a severe earthquake will have occurred in Turkey during the spring equinox; it will be the forerunner of several at the autumn equinox. The sad thing in the life of an astrologer when exploring the patterns relating to mundane matters is the frustration of being unable to do anything about the foreseeable results. Man has his free will to use or misuse, but there is an inexorable character about certain areas of life that man, no matter how forewarned he may be, can only accept and call destiny.

Meanwhile, the heavyweight planets Uranus, Neptune, and Pluto exert a more obvious influence than others on man and his environment.

The Los Angeles earthquake of February 9, 1971, added one more link in the chain of natural disasters that has been plaguing California. This state, like Florida, was named after the heroine of a now-forgotten novel about a medieval knight who wrested it by force from the gentle Indians living there. The dry, sunbaked hills frequently ran with blood, and it was usually Indian blood, not Spanish. The situation did not change much when Mexico broke away from the Spanish, carrying the territory of California with it. By the time California was dragged protestingly into the American corral, English-speaking "Anglos" were largely reduced to killing each other. California's political might grew, and so did the natural disasters. These disasters seem to have a strong relationship to aspects formed with Pluto, the planet of disruptions and drastic transformations. The passage of Pluto from Virgo into Libra seems to have had a powerfully negative astrological influence upon almost all aspects of Californian life.

During the morning of February 9, 1971, thousands of people in the southern part of the state were shaken from their beds by the worst earthquake in many, many years. Seers and mystics had been predicting this disaster for many years and astrologers had confirmed it. By 1971 the U.S.A. was entering a new high cycle when astrological references were applicable to just about everything. As the news of the earthquake came over the radios in the first bulletins, many people were asking themselves "What is the astrological meaning of all this?" A topical horoscope set up for the moment of this earthquake indicates a great deal to an astrologer, and when correlated to other events (even of a political nature), a dim pattern begins to emerge. Contemporary astrologers who for a long time had been like prophets crying in the wilderness were suddenly listened to. Confident of their success in predicting this earthquake, many have ventured farther afield in their speculations.

The earthquake and its astrological connotations also lead the astrologers into the field of politics. One basic and unmistakable trend that seems more and more clear is that there is less time between disasters in California. Each succeeding one will be more severe, and each time a different astrological "element" will be involved. During the February 9 earthquake, two elements were directly involved—namely, earth and water. (Earth, by the upheaval of the ground, and water, through the threatened flood of the cracked and broken dam.) This, also, had been foreseen for many years.

Despite good public relation services, there has been an exodus of people out of California, instead of an influx of people into the state. This will also have political repercussions in the coming years.

The great San Francisco earthquake of 1906 involved the astrological elements of earth and fire. Much of the city was destroyed by fire, and all succeeding disasters have always involved two of the astrological elements of earth, air, fire, and water. A growing number of astrologers interested in predicting earthquakes now seem to feel that "the really big one" foreseen by many adepts will bring into focus at least three, and possibly all four, of the elements. Enrico Caruso, the great and now legendary Italian tenor, was in San Francisco at the time of the 1906 earthquake. He never returned to the city, regardless of the temptation of high fees. When asked why, he replied, "When I looked out upon that dying city, God and His saints granted me a vision of the future and the coming death of this portion of America. And, I was looking into the jaws of hell itself!"

Shortly after the Second World War a point of no return was reached karmically for the whole region. The self-destructive cycle began to increase in tempo. What had once been known only to comparatively few adepts became the casual party conversation of many who merely knew of some of the vocabulary of mysticism, the occult, and astrology.

"Where can we go from here?" became more and more a
point of such conversations. One thing is certain: there is no
turning back the hands of the karmic clock. The debts of the
past, it seems, have to be paid, and it rests with each individual to attempt to solve his own individual, karmic, and astrological problems.

In order not to spread alarm and despondency in a state
already fraught with nervous and political tension, no one
now speaks of the time when "the big one" will hit California, but the eclipse in August 1971 was a time that was watched
with some concern by all contemporary astrologers. The next
California earthquake can be expected to be of truly cataclys-
mic dimensions, with unbelievably horrible fires and with
coastal areas being struck by tidal waves. There is also a very
strong and distinct possibility of a firestorm in the earthquake's hellish aftermath.

Automatically, the scientifically minded astrologer learns
to look for planetary patterns when studying a specific group
of people. Alan Leo studied groups of spiritually minded
people and helped to make the world aware of esoteric astrology; Carl Jung studied groups of people with regard to their
sexual and marital status; and Heinrich Daath produced a
great thesis on medical astrology by taking test groups of
people to ascertain the astrological reference to many of the
diseases that beset mankind. In every case, it is possible to see
dominating planetary patterns that show the causes leading
to the effects of esotericism, sexual deviations, and medical
problems.

Today the Age of Aquarius is on everyone's lips, but few
have a real idea of what it means. Life on this planet has always been divided into ages, and they last a little over two

thousand years. We are still in the Age of Pisces, which started at the birth of Jesus Christ and brought with it an entirely new form of religion and philosophic thoughts. No age occurs in just a single moment; there is a gradual moving toward it, a moving away from the old age. This is where we stand now, literally on the brink of the Age of Aquarius. Uranus, the planet of change, is the ruling planet of Aquarius, and we know that this is concerned with electricity and electrifying changes. Already we are moving toward an age of interplanetary travel as the space program takes men to the Moon, which in time will be a jumping-off point to other areas of space. We are also emerging into the computer age of highly involved forms of scientific invention.

No age dies easily. The pomp and ceremony of the Neptunian-ruled Piscean Age is still with us, but we can see the various establishments are fighting to survive, as we read of youth rioting against the establishment, of chaos in universities and areas of power. Neptune still tries to create its special brand of illusion, but young people who are going to mature in the year A.D. 2000 are likely to come to grips with the hallucinations of treacherous Neptune and give it the *coup de grace*, which will give Uranus the right to rule over its own age. There will be a completely new set of values—moral, religious, personal, and national—but the most important aspect is likely to be that groups of people will be more in evidence than the individual. The Aquarian Age will be democratic in principle but autocratic in actuality, and will probably involve a highly sophisticated form of police state in which groups of guardians keep a watchful eye on different parts of the Universe. Man will have to know what to do with his leisure time as more and more machines and computers

take over the everyday things of life. Because man has already gone through an age when material possessions were
meaningful as power structures, the new age will see a rever-
sal of this, with the mind dominating its material, the body.
Extrasensory perception will not be a way-out thing or a
conversation piece, but a viable asset and a part of the new
power structure. Exponents of ESP will literally have new
worlds to explore and to gradually gain control of. Mind over
matter will be the theme of the Aquarian Age, and mind will
perhaps even control a robotlike civilization such as we have
heard of in science fiction, and perhaps laughed about.

We should not approach this age with fear, therefore, but
with seriousness. We must have some new values prepared
before it is too late for individuals to be able to do anything
about them. In another two thousand years the Age of
Aquarius will give way to the Age of Capricorn, bringing an
unemotional sense of order in which we may well be in contact with entities on other planets and in other galaxies. But
the mind tuned in to astrology boggles a little at the thought
of the *next* age. Let us be realistic enough not to see the Age
of Aquarius as the answer to all the woes of the dying Piscean
Age. We shall simply be given a new set of standards, new
urges, and new problems—but man *will* be fitted to deal with
them.

Young astrologers have a great future before them. Their
position today is rather like that of psychologists some forty
years ago. At first, Freudians were unacceptable, but now are
completely accepted as performing a useful service to the
communities in which they work. There is no stigma today to
surgeons who do organ transplants, although they, too, were
once abused for interfering with nature. Chiropractors also

went through the same cycle of misunderstanding, but there are many who have reason to be thankful to chiropractors, and the same thankfulness is already being shown to astrologers. I almost envy the young astrologer learning his science, who will have so many years to practice in a world that must see astrology in its rightful context as a necessary tool to help man understand himself, his fellow men, and his place in the universe.

At various times of my life, I have sat down and assessed the value of all the major meaningful things in my own life. One, of course, is the Old Religion, which I have written about extensively, but the next major one is astrology. Through its disciplines I have found a new and more complete understanding of my fellow men. I have known compassion for the weaknesses of others as well as admiration for those who have survived the drastic effects of Saturn. I have seen Jupiter's influence increase the material wealth and the spiritual enlightenment of numerous people, and Venus manifest itself in a flow of beautiful and creative ideas. I have seen Pluto produce its own special type of people in the form of flower children, hippies, and yippies, and Uranus tear the earth asunder, and Neptune suddenly clarify deceptions as the unorthodox religions of the world seek to make themselves known and a new tide of personal enlightenment begins to flood through the world despite wars, chaos, and riots.

Most of all, I have lived long enough to feel the first effects of the Age of Aquarius. In seeking to extend my own knowledge of the influence of the planets on people and their behavior, I have found myself becoming a mature person able to cope with my own life and still having time to give help to others. This is where the satisfaction lies, and ultimately, this is what I call success.

The stars are linked to each other by attractions that hold them in equilibrium, causing them to move with regularity and rhythm through space. The network of their light stretches from all spheres to all spheres; there is not a point on any planet that is not attached to one of these indestructible threads. I think an astrologer becomes a technician who learns how to manipulate the threads for his own success and happiness and becomes joined to all other forces of nature on this planet, bathing in the various diffusions of light emanating from each planet. By understanding my own and other people's character, qualities, and capacities, I think I have come closer to the universe, and in the final analysis, have become a master of my own destiny.

This, perhaps, is the ultimate freedom we all seek. Astrology is a major tool in enabling us to find it.

So mote it be.